Asylum under dreaming spires

Refugees' lives in Cambridge today

Marella Hoffman

**In partnership with the Living Refugee Archive,
University of East London**

Other books by Marella Hoffman

Using oral history to improve public policies and programmes
Routledge, London, 2017

Savoir-faire des Anciens
- Un village des Corbières Maritimes, hier et demain
La Sorbonne University, Paris with Onslaught Press, Oxford, 2017
(Collectors' edition)

Savoir-faire des Anciens
- Un village des Corbières Maritimes, hier et demain
Cahiers de la Salce, France, 2016 (1st edition)

Magnets
Cambridge Editions, Cambridge, 2007

For Karmapa,

a refugee on the face of this earth

but at home in the universe

www.savetibet.org/resources/tibetan-refugees

Published in partnership with the Living Refugee Archive,
University of East London
Copyright © Marella Hoffman, 2017

A CIP catalogue record for this book is available from the British Library.
ISBN 978-0955-458651
Photos of Cambridge by Marella Hoffman
Others by Wikimedia Commons

The views expressed in this book are the author's own, not those of any organisation.

Printed and bound in Britain by CPI Books, Chatham, ME58TD

Words are all we have

Samuel Beckett, Irish playwright

'*Anyone could be a refugee. It's just something that happens to you. Nobody wants to leave their own country and risk dying at sea. But when it becomes impossible to live in your own country, you will do desperate things.*'

Syrian war-refugee Hassan Akkad,
one of the stars of Bafta-winning BBC film
Exodus - Our journey to Europe

Facebook *Hassan Akkad*

Thanks to

The speakers in this book, for opening to me their modest homes, big hearts and unforgettable stories

King's College, Cambridge University, who first invited me to this city for two years as a Visiting Scholar - without their generous hospitality I would never have come to this country, nor gotten to know the complex, elusive populations who mingle here

Norma Buckley, my mother, whose work with her own community in Ireland is part of our shared interest in place, and who has always loved Cambridge

Local government in Cambridge, for the many projects and publications we did together as part of their ongoing work to redress inequalities

The Living Refugee Archive, University of East London, for giving this project and these voices a home

Foreword

Paul V. Dudman and Rumana Hashem [1]

Those who experience the refugee journey are, on the one hand, marginalised from the community history that they leave behind, and on the other, often remain invisible to the community history in their place of integration. There is a dearth of documentation on migrants' and refugees' lived experience, and on the original history of migration.

Neither academics nor third sector advocates have adequately engaged with the collation, documentation and preservation of the history of refugees in the UK. Commentators Laybourn and Hughes have correctly noted that the academic study of migration history has been 'in the doldrums' [2] for too long as a peripheral area of concern within the discipline of history. [3] It is time to focus on the collection and preservation of the original history of refugees and migrants.

Marella Hoffman's new book, *Asylum under dreaming spires - Refugees' lives in Cambridge today*, does this. The book engages with the local refugee community and presents excerpts of original interviews collated through oral recordings, allowing us to recognise the voices of refugees and the original histories of refugees in Cambridge.

The book is important for its originality and for the oral history testimonies of refugees who undergo hostility in a supposedly multicultural state of Britain. The collection of oral narratives and their subsequent accession into archival collections can play an important role in helping to restore this migration history. The lived experiences and memories of migrants and refugees in Cambridge can add voices to the existing historical narratives of migrants in the UK. Oral history testimonies can go a long

---

[1] Paul V. Dudman is archive director at the University of East London (UEL). Dr. Rumana Hashem is a post-doctoral researcher at UEL's Centre for Refugees, Migration and Belonging. Dudman and Hashem run UEL's *Living Refugee Archive*.

[2] Laybourn, K. & Hughes, R.,2006. Twentieth Century. *Annual Bulletin of Historical Literature* , 90 (1), pp. 133-157

[3] Burrell, K. & Panayi, P., 2006. Introduction - Immigration and British History. In: *Histories and Memories - Migrants and their Histories in Britain*. London: I.B. Tauras

way to redressing the imbalance in historical study which has overlooked for too long the impact of *community* history, within the wider narratives of local and national history.

Oral narrative has been increasingly recognised by social scientists as a powerful tool for understanding the lived experiences of lay people. Recording the lived experiences and memories of refugees - whose lives are routinely shaped and reshaped within the wider history of the communities into which they are integrating - is significant for preserving the history both of refugees and of migration. Through the collection of oral narratives told by refugees themselves, we can begin to make their original voices more accessible. In fact, the oral recording of such narratives can be reflective of the process of integration within a new host community. We can highlight the difficulties associated with the migration process and the multi-layering of identity which occurs as a consequence of trying to integrate within a new host community.

Marella Hoffman's *Asylum under dreaming spires - Refugees' lives in Cambridge today* is therefore a timely work which highlights the importance of collecting and preserving first-hand testimonies through the medium of oral history recordings. The oral narratives in this book may appear unedited, but it is useful to have testimonies in this undistorted form because it highlights the often complex interplay of identities experienced by refugees and asylum seekers during their experience of flight and integration.

As researchers, and as a community activist and archivist in the field of migration and refugee studies, we are pleased to be able to write the foreward to this book. The opportunity to collaborate on the publication of this work came about as a result of a civic engagement project that we were working on between the spring and summer of 2015. Our civic engagement project, funded by a small grant from the University of East London, aimed to engage with local refugee communities through personal networking, collation of oral history, and the creation of the website of the Living Refugee Archive. The research on refugee oral history in London and the now established Living Refugee Archive would, we hoped, be the first step in making the University of East London's archival collections more accessible, taking them beyond the narrow confines of academia.

It was during this time that the author of *Asylum under dreaming spires - Refugees' lives in Cambridge today*, nearing the completion of her project to collect oral history testimonies from refugees in Cambridge, began investigating the possibility of where the finished material could be housed. A conference at University of East London's Centre for Migration, Refugees and Belonging brought us together and the work that you see in front of you now is a culmination of our subsequent collaborative work.

This book is a timely work which documents the voices of the refugees themselves, and helps to contextualise the refugee histories recorded within these narratives into the wider history of the communities into which they are integrating.

Living Refugee Archive, University of East London

May 2016

Introduction

Marella Hoffman

Why listen to refugees?

This book's narratives will lead you into the bizarre, ritualistic heart of the ancient city of Cambridge, England - city of dreaming spires - and then on many technicolour journeys over the high seas. [4] You'll be carried out onto the great swells of the South China Sea, into the folds of the hills of Kurdistan, through the sun-soaked manor estates of Southern Africa. In each chapter, a refugee will tell you in their own words how they came to be living in Cambridge.

Circumstances herded them here involuntarily from Asia, Africa, the Middle East, Eastern Europe, and even Western Europe. So each chapter opens onto another world - the experiences of displaced people who rub shoulders with us every day in cities like Cambridge. The last chapter erupted - unsolicited - into the book after the manuscript was already finished. I will leave you to discover its fairly breathtaking events for yourself.

There is of course a huge media spotlight these days on the politics and logistical challenges around newly-arrived refugees - those risking their lives to be trafficked across the Mediterranean to Italy or Greece; those squatting in Calais trying to get illicit transport into the UK; those awaiting asylum-decisions in various host countries…

But those moments are just that - *moments* - snapshots in a refugee journey that is actually much longer, often lasting a lifetime. Each refugee's individual drama has distinct *before*, *during* and *after* phases that play out over a much longer time-frame. The most dramatic phase is also the shortest - the crisis of fleeing from home and seeking asylum elsewhere. And it is understandable that that is a focus for the public and media. But any credible solution to the burgeoning challenges that the world will face

---

[4] Oxford, and later Cambridge, became known as the cities of 'dreaming spires', after the phrase appeared in a poem by Matthew Arnold in 1861.

around refugees in the years ahead must also include a much deeper understanding and integration of what went *before* for them - what lifestyles, skills, attitudes and assets they had before being displaced. And it is increasingly urgent that we also understand and engage deeply with the *afterwards* - the life they will try to piece together once settled in a host country, and the attitudes, integrations and contributions that they will go on to develop there.

So how well *do* they manage to integrate into host societies? How much do they want to integrate anyway? Are some host cultures more difficult to integrate into than others? What makes the difference between just being physically and economically settled - and feeling genuinely a part of one's adoptive nation? These questions are not only about the long-term welfare and economics of settled refugees, nor just about finding ways to calm the xenophobic tensions rising around migrants in western countries. The security forces are also increasingly recognising that these questions are critical to the safety and security of the host society. Crime statistics show that the vast majority of refugees are peaceful and law-abiding. But we do know that many of the terrorist attacks in western countries in recent years were organised by first or second generation migrants who had failed to integrate with the values or civic identity of their host countries.

For these and other reasons, this book delves into the *afterwards* experienced by refugees who were granted asylum and set about building new lives here in England. As a reality check, it asks those who have been settled here for some time how they feel now about English society, and how they feel about their country of origin. What do they feel their civic identity is now, and what is their experience of the host society?

Methodology and partnerships

I have in the past worked as an academic at Cambridge University and on policy for city government in Cambridge, but I did this book project with refugees entirely as an independent researcher. This independent research was designed to yield a range of applied, transdisciplinary outcomes that were subsequently delivered by local authorities. These policy actions ensured the project had a concrete and measurable positive impact on local communities, beyond the covers of this book.

So the project has moved through three phases and multiple media: they are explained in detail in the conclusion and appendix so that readers can use such strategies for their own projects if they wish. The first phase, over a period of eighteen months, was my collection of oral histories from refugees settled in Cambridge. The second phase was a multi-media programme of anti-racist and diversity trainings that I designed using insights, learnings and suggestions gleaned from the interviews. Using these, I was employed by local government to design and deliver:

- a programme of trainings and public events to raise awareness both among refugees and among the host communities around them

- political empowerment and roles within the democratic system for refugees and other ethnic minority residents

- a range of other policy outcomes that got implemented by the local authority [5]

The final phase of the project was partnering with the Living Refugee Archive at the University of East London (UEL), which is committed to opening up links between refugee archives and embedded community projects on the ground. The mission of the Living Refugee Archive is to 'preserve and make accessible the history and heritage of the refugee experience' and to 'promote accessibility and civic engagement through working in the heart of local communities to deliver solutions to the challenges they face'. So this book is produced in partnership with the Living Refugee Archive and will be available there as part of a resource pack providing support, methodologies, ideas and inspiration for anyone interested in doing a similar project, however big or small. The resource pack contains:

---

[5] This programme of awareness-raising and work towards equality was commended in the national policy press by the head of the government's Audit Commission, who cited it as one of the country's most innovative approaches to diversity and equality. (Irwin, R., 2009. Ten ways to get diversity right. *Inside Housing Journal*, 4-10-2009)

- this book, whose appendix gives a 'How-To' guide for community action in its Appendix, with strategies that readers can use for running their own events with grassroots communities

- my accompanying book *Hidden gold - Using contemporary oral history to improve public policies and programmes* (Routledge, 2017), itself a 'How-To' manual showing how oral histories can be used to consult communities, involve them in public policy and achieve better outcomes for those communities

- a Powerpoint presentation summarising the socio-political data extracted from the oral interviews in this book [6]

- my contact details: I can be contacted at any time, as a partner of the Living Refugee Archive, for advice on how to do a similar project of your own

In this way we can all, through our partnerships, build up a body of practice where applied community projects actively learn from each other and inspire further outcomes.

Applied, transdisciplinary research

The purpose of this project has been to do qualitative research that gets translated into applied, transdisciplinary impacts for communities. It has done this by:

- building bridges and mutual learning between grassroots communities, academic archives and public policy-makers

- addressing issues in engaging, multi-disciplinary ways, free of academic jargon

- applying the learning from the interviews back into the community in practical ways that make a measurable difference to ordinary people's lives

6 Called 'Dilemmas of belonging and resistance - Refugee voices in Cambridge', it was presented at a conference on *Evolving understandings of racism and resistance - local and global conceptions and struggles* at the Centre for Migration, Refugees and Belonging, University of East London, May 2015

- ensuring that the project's learnings are *generative*, seeding new projects for others and supporting them to spread further community learning

To help build these inclusive bridges, the book and project incorporated five different types of information and perspective:

1. The majority of the book is in the *direct speech* of the refugees, their interviews edited only for length, and for anonymity where needed.

2. The introduction and conclusion give brief *sociological analyses* of the political, cultural and economic dynamics that have shaped the refugees' responses to England as a host society.

3. The book as a whole and each interview within it are book-ended with brief commentaries from me as an ethnographer. The *ethnographic approach* involves turning the lens back on the researcher to reveal how their own class, ethnicity, politics, profession and migration status colour the lens through which they see their environment and interviewees. It also means observing and decoding some of the physical spaces, cultural practices, power structures, material objects and social rituals encountered while doing outreach and interviews.

4. The book uses *multi-media* to convey different types of information. The ethnographic passages have a novelistic, almost filmic quality, and the interviews are illustrated with photos, graphic icons and oral proverbs from the speakers' home-cultures. The appendix explains how our subsequent policy actions used journalism, theatre, role-play, games, dance, costume, food and art exhibits to embed learnings in the community.

5. As mentioned above, the book's conclusion and appendix include a practical *How-To guide* for community action, with strategies readers can use for running their own events with grassroots communities, as we did. There are also signposts to further guides and resources, both on gathering oral histories and on community applications for oral history.

The speakers

Before doing interviews, I first did a phase of ethnographic outreach, making contact with the city's ethnic communities and building trust with individuals among them. I was looking for speakers whose life histories would be representative, who were willing and able to tell me their stories, and were engaging to listen to.

It was important that I did the interviews as an independent researcher, as such openness from the refugees would not have been possible within my other professional roles. They knew I had worked at Cambridge University and city government in the past but it was crucial that I came to the interviewees independently in my own time, bringing with me only my training as an ethnographer. This is quite different from viewing interviewees through an academic or institutional lens, which I've done in both those other roles. By contrast, the desire of the ethnographic listener is to hear *the speaker's own expertise about their own world*. This has quite a powerful effect on the openness and content of interviews.

The speakers knew I would publish their interviews, and were very keen indeed to have their voices heard. But for reasons that become clear in each interview, almost all needed anonymity so they could speak with total openness for the first time ever, which they passionately wished to do. For the same reasons, some needed their precise country of origin not to be identifiable, though the geographical region is clear. [7]

As part of the early ethnographic outreach, I spent months meeting and interviewing much wider circles of refugees and migrants. I then selected the interviewees for this book from among them, to give the broadest possible diversity in terms of age, class, marital status, work status, finances, education, religion and political views. So they range from PhDs to complete illiteracy; from religious practitioners to atheists; from a state of starvation in the country of origin to extreme affluence there; and from being political campaigners to avoiding all contact with politics. They are, variously, single, married, divorced, with or without children, unemployed,

---

[7] Cambridge is a small city with a 'Town' population of only about 100,000, alongside the University's 'Gown' population of 25,000. So an interviewee giving both their life story and country of origin would be easily identifiable inside the town's close-knit ethnic minority communities.

working or retired. The religious come from Muslim, Buddhist and Christian backgrounds, as well as from various sects within those religions.

Yet despite all this diversity, the single thing they had most in common was the fact that they had all fallen dramatically in financial status between leaving their home country and landing in England. Back home, most had comfortable, middle-class lives. They had professions, owned properties and enjoyed a meaningful role in their society. When they had to abandon all that, most of them fell very steeply indeed, financially. Thus the international diplomat, the court solicitor and the IT consultant back home became penniless and unemployed here. The comfortable farm-owner back home became a miner in the English coal-pits. Only one of them saw their financial status improved by coming here: you will see that she rose from starvation back home to earning her living working three jobs as a domestic cleaner in Cambridge.

This illustrates some of the critical differences between refugees and economic migrants. None of these interviewees had wanted to come here: they weren't seeking a 'better life'. They all wanted the normal lives they had back in their own cultures. But those lives became impossible, ripped away by three things they had to flee from just to stay alive: war, persecutory regimes or sexual persecution. Four of the ten fled from wars. Four others fled imprisonment and torture for opposing corrupt regimes. And two fled the religious strictures around sexuality that were enforced by their country's courts and police.

All this is typical of the big-picture statistics about asylum in the UK. But one of the most surprising things in these first-hand accounts - where for once we get to hear the real-life narratives behind those statistics - is that for most, it was a single dramatic moment that turned their existence upside down and meant they had to flee from their homes: a betrayal, a lie, an abandonment, a violent incident, a protection removed... Or else it was a rising tide of persecution that reached a tipping-point in the course of one night. Or a moment when it became clear that finally now, after years of fine-balancing the risks and benefits, it was more deadly to stay than to run.

You couldn't make it up, this level of human drama. The stolen watch that changed the whole course of a lifetime. The life betrayed by a single invented lie. The young hunger-striker who died quietly next morning... It's all here in these chapters.

But there are hilarious and uplifting moments too - these people did not survive without a sense of humour. There's the interviewee who found work as a bus-conductor here, but showed he came from a cultured background by whistling classical music and speaking French to tourists. There were the jeeps driving out into the African bush to ferry tribespeople in to vote in the first democratic elections. There is a death-bed apology.

Some of the interviewees tell these life-changing moments vividly: they *want* them recorded once and for all. Others pass over the detail of how their last days at home unfolded, as being too painful or dangerous to revisit. To be granted asylum they will already have had to tell the full, gory detail to many official decision-makers and fact-checkers. Some do not want to go over it all again. And the pain is compounded by the fact that for the great majority of them, the war, repression, corruption and unrest that drove them from their home country has escalated dramatically behind them since they left, and even since we started this project.

Corrupt regimes back home form a permanent backdrop to their accounts, whether the persecutions they had to flee were military, political or sexual. But it is heartening to hear almost all of them describe a basic fairness - kindness, even - in the many officials they have had to deal with here in England. The interviews describe English medical staff, housing officers, job-centre staff and librarians as decent, level-headed people who often 'go the extra mile' to humanise or simplify the system for a refugee in difficulty.

A new life in England?

But gratitude is a complex issue for refugees. Their feelings about their new life are much more ambivalent than those of economic migrants, who choose to make a migration they feel will benefit them. Refugees, by contrast, having lost so much, seem at first to feel mainly grief and trauma in this alien place. Yet they know intellectually that they are supposed to feel 'lucky' to have been rescued from death or worse back home by this

British government who decided to take them in - to save them - for purely humanitarian reasons. Like the sole survivors of a shipwreck, they know they should feel grateful for being plucked onto one of the few places on the life-boat. But - not least because relatives, friends and compatriots are often still trapped in the old regime back home - newly-arrived refugees find it hard to rejoice about their un-chosen migration, though the interviews show that time does bring some healing, if only through resignation.

Like so many people beyond the English-speaking world, the interviewees spoke an average of three languages each, though most knew no English before arriving here. (They had never planned to come here.) How quickly they were able to learn perfect English was a major factor in their employability. And their longing for work seemed a constant, burning theme. Refugees seem to desire work with a fervour unmatched even by economic migrants. With many, I got the sense that work felt like the only possible salvation - the only possible medicine - when to sit undistracted would be to be overwhelmed by all the bad memories, and the memories of the good things lost.

The highly qualified refugees that I met - lawyers, scientists, academics, journalists, film-makers - seemed to suffer most, because it would be so much harder for them to regain their lost professions here than it is to find manual labour here. To stand a chance of regaining their profession here, they would first need perfect professional English, full mental and physical health, evidence of qualifications officially adapted to meet the requirements of the English version of their profession, and a receptive network of peer contacts opening doors for them into the profession here. Among certain refugee nationalities, I seemed to meet a disproportionate number of these professionals. I understand this to be because a) professionals like lawyers, journalists, academics and film-makers are more likely to pose an oppositional threat to corrupt regimes and hence to be targeted by them, and b) they have the financial means to flee from their home-country if they need to.

Whatever their social class back home, all the interviewees connect up with their compatriots here for support and solidarity. They do this through extended family and clan networks, if relatives or neighbours from home have also migrated to this country. And they do it through churches, mosques, clubs and cultural celebrations as well as through business-networks, where compatriots assist each other to find and sustain work and housing. This is a well-documented norm for ethnic communities in the UK.

Conflicting solidarities

But in the course of the interviews it also becomes clear that for refugees in particular, four different types of conflict undercut this potential solidarity provided by their own ethnic networks. Firstly, there may be radical class-divides carried over from 'back home': if estate-owners and the starving didn't have a lot in common back in their home country, they may not have a lot in common here either, even if refugee displacement has levelled their economic status to being more similar now.

Secondly, compatriots are sometimes divided over the complexities of how to respond to racism and segregation here - the choices of whether to ignore racism and turn inward to the compatriot community, or to challenge it overtly, or to try to leave ethnic identities behind altogether and blend into native English culture (a near-impossible task, the interviewees explain, because they feel native English residents don't generally want to share this 'Englishness' with them).

For refugees as opposed to other migrants, these issues of integration are especially complicated by the fact that they hadn't wished to leave their home in the first place. They tend to arrive destitute in the new country, at first entirely dependent on the host community, whereas they often had successful, independent lifestyles back home. Economic migrants, on the other hand, tend to arrive with a plan, some resources and connections, and an appetite for getting stuck in immediately to a labour market that they see as rewarding - their prime motivation for coming here in the first place.

In the interviews, I deliberately did not raise the subject of racism or ask whether they had experienced it: I wanted to see whether they would raise it themselves unprompted. By the book's conclusion, you'll know the sometimes surprising things they said about it, and we'll review their thoughts on racism.

A third factor inhibiting interviewees from relying much on a compatriot network can be the fact that for some, their community back home, whether poor or wealthy, was a multi-ethnic, multi-religion, multi-lingual environment where they were used to mingling with a very diverse range of people. This cosmopolitanism that they were used to leaves them averse to a mono-ethnic strategy of hunkering down with just their own narrow ethnic group here, which they tend to feel they are expected to do by the English.

Interestingly, some of the interviewees are disappointed not to find in England the cosmopolitan, melting-pot society that they were used to in their own country. They describe disliking the English 'multi-cultural' approach which, though touted as 'tolerant', encourages minorities to cluster in self-sufficient ghettos with their own ethnicity, functioning as mini-societies within the larger English nation. Some speakers describe how strange and alienating that feels to them.

They express their disappointment at this 'separate communities' approach and the lack of invitation to *join in* with native English culture and *'become English'*, participating fully in specifically English culture and practices. Some of them know that this question of integration is approached differently in neighbouring countries. Examples are in France or Scandinavia, where citizenship is lived as a very clear set of public, cultural practices that all residents are expected to participate in together and adopt cohesively, regardless of ethnic or financial background.

In my own view, the reason this doesn't happen in England is that the model of 'living separate lives' applies not only between native and immigrant communities here but also between the severely stratified classes of the native English themselves. Both as a foreigner and an ethnographer, I've noticed that the public rituals and festivals of English culture seem to have the function of *fortifying* the demarcation-lines between these stratified native classes. (English football, TV soaps and tabloids are the territory of the working classes. Cheltenam, Henley, Wimbledon, the Chelsea Flower Show, the Proms and the National Trust are for the middle and upper classes. And neither of these demographics seem to wish to stray into each other's cultural territory...)

Public culture often has the opposite function in nearby countries such as Spain, Italy and Ireland, where food-culture, music or sporting festivals have a powerfully assimilating effect: they are designed to cut strategically across class and background, unifying the population in a calendar of collective rituals across the year. [8] Divergences of wealth, class, education, politics and even ethnicity - though real and present - are muted into the background by these festivals, rather than being underscored and reinforced by them, as English public rituals tend to do.

A fourth complication in refugees' relationship to their compatriot networks here is ideological disagreement about political conflicts and regimes back home, whether past or present. In fact, politics seem to be the biggest disruptor of compatriot relations for the interviewees. These ongoing divergences - revealed when exiled compatriots regroup for support and solidarity here - emerge in the interviews as a surprisingly painful aspect of refugee life. Political or ideological disagreements within their own nationality don't magically melt away when they meet here. And feelings are strong because these very politics may well be the reason the refugee had to flee from their country in the first place.

Such divergences include, for instance, how Chinese people living here feel about the Chinese government's human rights record back home; how Muslim women here feel about women's life under Sharia law; how Turkish people here feel about Kurdish identity; how Irish people here feel about Northern Ireland's colonial status and the 'Troubles' there… These internal conflicts between compatriot groups tend to be more inflammatory than any frictions they could have with other nationalities. A recurrent theme in the interviews is the way the speakers have to navigate these painful rifts within their own communities here.

A related question is refugees' level of political activity once they settle in this country. Do they mobilise here about political issues back in the

---

[8] Specifically, this is the case for food-culture in Spain and Italy, and for sporting festivals and music in Spain and Ireland.

home country? Do they vote and get involved in party politics here? How active are they on themed, international political issues like sexual politics, class, trade unionism or immigration politics? For now we will let the interviews answer these questions, and we'll review their responses in our conclusion. I will just say in advance here that, for reasons that will become clear in the interviews, their level of political activism turns out to be as low as that of the general population here, but their level of civic activism and community engagement is much higher than that of the general population. In the interviews, we will hear why.

Their many volunteering activities include supporting churches, charities, schools, residents' associations, parent and toddler groups, community centres, advice services, language classes and computer classes. Their interventions range from firefighting and helping the elderly to volunteering with the local council or NHS services. Given the political and social dilemmas listed above, one can see why civil society engagement might feel more attractive to refugees than overt political campaigning. These speakers are clearly still keen to 'give back' something practical to society. And civic activism may also help them to feel less displaced and devalued, now that their options for making the professional and financial contributions they used to make back home may be severely limited.

Talking about 'England'

I refer to the host-nation wrapped around us here in Cambridge as *England*. I'm acutely aware that academics, the media, politicians, public sector professionals and the middle-classes in this country - in other words, all the colleagues I've ever had here - have an intense preference for using the term *Britain* instead. On arriving to live here, I was amazed to discover how deeply uncomfortable these parts of the population are about referring to their own country by its own name, preferring to mask it behind the aggregating 'group-hug' term *Britain* that includes the three Celtic colonies still governed by London. Here are the five main reasons why I haven't succumbed to the pressure to do the same.

A feeble claim to political correctness is the justification colleagues give me for never mentioning England, only *Britain*: they lamely tell me that

Scotland, Wales, Ireland and this islands' various immigrants from elsewhere would all be (mysteriously) 'offended' if Englanders referred to their own part of the island as England. The first problem with this - a thorny issue that could not be clearer to the Celtic, colonised and immigrant peoples above who are looking on - is that the concept of *Britain* is in reality not a group-hug between equals, but rather what's left over from the otherwise disbanded British Empire. It never was a federated union of equal regions like, say, the USA or Switzerland. *Britain* came about by the three other nations being militarily invaded, brutally land-cleared and occupied by the armies and settlers of an expansionist England. Today, those territories have settled around their coloniser in three different, nuanced, pragmatic relationships that range from mutual benefit (currently being reassessed by Scotland) to the impotent dependency of the war-broken Northern Ireland, now sustained at considerable cost by the coloniser.

The second problem with insisting on the term *Britain* - refusing to let England and the three other regions each speak for or about themselves - is that the other three countries are so diametrically different from England in their cultures, languages, history, economics, politics and attitudes. But it often seems that Anglocentricity is so clouding a force on this bottom half of the island that it's hard for the English to see or acknowledge the profundity of cultural differences to the north and west.

Outside this cloud of Anglocentricity, the reality is that the three other countries are Celtic, colonised, largely rural, poorer, peripheralised cultures with three different, entirely foreign languages and an emphasis on oral traditions. [9] By contrast, England's experience and politics have been as an Anglo-Saxon, colonising, expansionist, English language-spreading, world economic power and, traditionally, a world player politically too. These four nations can certainly dialogue and get on, but it's ridiculous not to recognise

---

[9]   These languages shape fundamentally different worldviews. For instance the Irish language, though notoriously complex, has no possessive verb that simply means *to own or possess*. Instead, the language conveys the concept in subtler terms of relationship, contiguity and impermanence, as opposed to the blander English concept of ownership as lasting dominance. In Irish you can only say that something - this cup/ house/ husband - is *'with me'* or *'in association to me'*, rather than I *'have'* or *'possess'* it (ie. *'tá cupán/ teach/ fear chéile agam'*).

the depth of their cultural differences, something foreigners have no trouble doing when they look at these countries.

The fourth problem with English thinkers insisting on a single, supposedly unified identity of *Britain* for these four countries is that this tends to be a cloak for the Anglocentric voice, where England as the dominant culture is actually insisting on speaking for the other three, through the voice of 'Britain'.

Free of the centrifugal force that is Anglocentricity, foreigners see these differences between the four countries much more easily. Irish people, for instance, have always referred to this country quite simply as England - never as 'Britain' - because they have an intense, first-hand awareness of how different its culture is from that of Scotland, Ireland or Wales. (In addition, most Irish people never thought of this country's empire as a good thing.) Meanwhile, the nearest neighbours on the other side, the French, are equally clear-eyed in referring to this country as *Angleterre*, England. They instantly recognise its culture as being deeply different from that of *l'Ecosse*, Scotland - as different as France is from Spain.

The fifth problem is that in many ways, all parties both at home and abroad are in fact much clearer about the identity of countries like Scotland and Ireland than any of us are about that of England. Who is England now, when it's not hiding behind the group-hug 'Britain'? What is its culture? What is it like to live in it?

But remember that it's only the English themselves who don't want to talk about 'England': the foreigners speaking in this book are more than happy to do so. They are vividly aware that the specifically English culture and society that they are trying to settle into (remember, *Anglo-Saxon coloniser with a world metropolis*) is a diametrically different host-culture than the one they would be entering if settling in Scotland or Northern Ireland (*Celtic, colonised, with Gaelic worldviews...*). So the speakers in this book have a great deal to say, unprompted, about the specificity of Englishness, and what it is like for outsiders to live here.

The human voice

Apart from practical contributions to society, perhaps the greatest thing any human being can offer is their story - their own unique voice in the world. In African and Middle Eastern cultures, oral traditions have often had a higher status than words that are merely written. In those societies, the naked human voice - talking, singing or chanting while others listen closely - has long been the basis of public narratives, ancestral memory and traditional law. In Ireland, where I grew up, conversation is still the most prized and exalted activity, undimmed by the fact that Ireland is now a very high-tech, internet-savvy society. Both the telling and the listening are still considered the highest form of entertainment.

English tradition and values tend to be the opposite. Here for almost a thousand years the official, written word has enjoyed a much higher status than the simple human voice. England has long been famous the world over for its written codes and canons - in its literature, universities, exam-systems and codes of law and government. And the small, wealthy city of Cambridge is of course, along with Oxford, an epicentre of that proud tradition of *written* knowledge.

The day I first arrived to live in Cambridge, the thing that immediately struck me most was not the dreaming spires of the architecture but the relatively low status of conversation in English culture. As an ethnographer, it was fascinating to encounter this famous conversational reserve that I had only heard about before, described as the English 'stiff upper lip'. Several of the interviewees here comment that English people seem particularly uninterested in listening and deep conversation. (As these things are relative, they mean, of course, compared to people in the other cultures that they were used to.) I too was very struck by this resistance to in-depth conversation when I first arrived in Cambridge. In the two cultures I was coming from (rural Irish society, and Parisian universities and cafe-culture), daily, *probing*, face to face conversation and animated debate were absolutely central to society, and a high-status activity. There, it was considered rude *not* to talk.

In my first weeks and months in Cambridge, I encountered the opposite. Initially baffled, one quickly learned by observation or rebuke that the most high-status, valued behaviour was to be *reserved*, saying as little as possible about yourself, your experiences, opinions, emotions, origins and aspirations. This extended equally to not asking others about themselves in any depth, nor provoking situations where they might feel invited to disclose anything about themselves.

In Ireland, to be reserved, silent or apparently uninterested like that is a very low-status behaviour that would quickly exile you from all social groups and make you an object of suspicion. And French people - Parisians in particular - are notoriously, challengingly direct. Sex, relationships, political passions, interpersonal feuds - it's all fodder and entertainment for heated dinner-table discussions. [10] So I understood viscerally the frustration described in the interviews by people coming from cultures that put a high value on orality. In trying to privately explain to themselves this baffling English reserve, you'll see that the interviewees' explanations for it range from amnesia and indifference to repression, superiority and parochialism.

In fact, it's not just in oral cultures but all over the world now that there is a growing awareness of the importance of oral testimony. Whether in politics, war, law or community relations, oral accounts are restoring voice to the dispossessed, revealing the perspectives of those who may have lost all other material advantage and power. Oral testimonies can bypass and challenge the hegemonic statements of official institutions, media, and commercial and political lobbies that defend their own interests. As even poorer communities gain access to the internet and social media, expressing themselves in the public domain, our concepts of knowledge are becoming more democratic. All over the world, younger generations no longer tolerate the notion that 'truth' and 'knowledge' are the exclusive domain of the elite professions and classes, academics and government. The old hierarchies of knowledge are flattening out.

In the global village, it's increasingly recognised that the embedded individual and their local microcosm are at least as likely to hold key knowledge and solutions as are the distant authorities. This approach respects the grounded, informal oral expertise of communities. It

---

[10] Anthropologist Kate Fox explores these English 'conversation codes' at length in her highly readable ethnography of English culture, called *Watching the English - The hidden rules of English behaviour*, Hodder & Stoughton, 2014

acknowledges that elites - governments, corporations, top bosses, technology experts, academics - no longer have all the answers, or enough answers. It recognises that elite forces have dragged us into environmental disaster, global economic crisis, the growing divide between rich and poor, and the health crises derived from western lifestyles. So we need more participative approaches - techniques that also listen to the needs and wishes of the ordinary people who are, after all, the majority. [11]

As well as being used to improve policy, refugees' oral testimonies can also awaken our humanity. They shift us from viewing the refugee as a mere statistic (the way we usually hear about them *en masse* in the media), to meeting them as an individual human being who carries inside them a whole world of motivations, attitudes and emotions - in addition to the dramatic narrative of danger and displacement that they are living on the outside.

Even after the most chaotic aspects of that displacement have been settled, as in the case of the speakers in this book who all have leave to stay in this country, the turbulent emotions left behind often need airing before the refugee can move forward into a productive, progressive life in the host country. On issues as diverse as migration, religion, sexual politics, foreign policy, citizenship and terrorism, western policy-makers have suddenly woken up to the urgent need to *hear and understand* these perspectives of our migrant and ethnic populations - with the tardy realisation that they don't fully understand them. That is why the interviews in this book asked: 'Tell us: how has it all been for you?' And in fact the interviewees wanted very much to tell us, but no-one had ever asked.

The oral history interview is fundamentally different from the many other sorts of interviews that refugees will have experienced. They go through medical interviews that dig into their health history; police interviews and interrogations, both in the UK and the home country (though hopefully more humanely here); legal interviews where lawyers extract information to build them a case, or to oppose their case; assessment interviews for jobs, benefits or housing; research interviews

---

[11] As mentioned earlier, my book on this subject, *Hidden gold - Using oral history to shape public policy*, will be published in 2017 by Routledge.

where tick-boxes count them up as a diversity statistic; media interviews where journalists pump them for quotes… Because newly-arrived refugees are total outsiders, they have to be actively 'processed' like this into every layer of our socio-economic structures, which they cannot penetrate or navigate through by themselves. So refugees get interviewed *a lot*.

But the oral history interview is different in three main ways. First, it rests on a redistribution of the usual power structure, with the speaker given much more power to define for themselves the content and the limits of what they choose to tell us. Secondly, there is more empathic awareness, with the listener centring appreciation and respect on the speaker as an expert who has something of universal and community value to tell. Thirdly, this in turn creates a gently performative quality, where the speaker is centre-stage and can relax in the full attention of an appreciative listener.

All the interviewees in this book are eloquent. But for the ones whose past was violent, it can be difficult to find the words to tell of those experiences, especially here in a foreign culture and language, among people who know nothing about the regime that brutalized them. Very often interviewees told me it was rare it was for them to feel truly *listened to* - listened to with interest and respect, at length - and how they had longed for that listening. Many did not even feel the need or desire to see their story handed back to them in written form, when I offered it. They just wanted to be deeply listened to once and for all, and to get that story told as fully as they personally could.

So to celebrate the orality that has been the central focus of this project, each speaker's chapter opens with a proverb or quote from their country's oral culture. Remember that such proverbs are essentially oral *teaching devices* - little capsules of meaning that transmit a culture's values across the generations. They often neatly convey the psychology and behaviours that are valued in a particular society. So as you read the proverb that opens each interview, I invite you to wonder what it conveys about the culture it comes from.

Let's embark now on these many journeys. Photos at the beginning of each chapter depict aspects of the speaker's story that will unfold as you read their interview. [12]

 Throughout the book, this microphone marks the voices of the refugee speakers.

 And my brief comments before and after their interviews are marked with this little note-board that I carried with me.

---

[12] For anonymity, most of the faces in the photos are not those of the interviewees themselves but of people who look like them. However, the photos of Stefan on page 156 and of Kanwar and his baby Daniel on page 188 are really of them.

Arriving...

Glancing at the clipboard of notes on the lectern in front of me, I start to speak. This is what I'm here to do. I've just arrived from Paris to take up a position at Cambridge University, and I've been invited to give a lecture on one of my specialist areas - life in cities. Specifically, on the *flâneur*, that outsider figure (originally in Paris but later in any city) who wanders through the back-streets, noticing and writing about things that others ignore. The students' eyes fix on me, glittering and avid. With exams looming, they hover between focus and panic - little Rottweilers of the intellect, hungry for any titbit that could claw a few extra marks.

This is the first time I've been to England. I arrived last week, invited to King's College, Cambridge, as a Visiting Scholar for the next two years. I'm asking myself the questions I always ask when arriving to live in a new country. (As a young academic I've already worked in Ireland, France and Switzerland.) What are these people like, in this culture? What is the *story* they collectively tell about themselves? What are their symbols and rituals? What identity makes them tick?

After the lecture I attend *Evensong* ceremony in King's College Chapel, wearing the black college robes that apparently I must wear. (The butler slithered up to me with a robe over his arm when I went to walk in without one.)

I'm reclining in the ancient polished stalls, tall candles flickering above me. It's fun observing the strangeness of all this, like watching a foreign film. I got my academic training from the pavestone-throwing, left-wing French intellectuals who led the cultural revolution of *Paris 1968* - libertines, poets, revolutionaries, psychoanalysts... The medieval rituals of these academics here seem alien as a dream.

Sitting there admiring the almighty stained-glass windows, I assume that I know my own future. I'll stay just one academic year in this weird place - not two as planned - and move on, like a bird flying through on a long, lazy migration. Go back to work in France, spend a couple of years in the States and then settle in Ireland, where I grew up. With the arrogance of youth, I do not realise that I don't hold the knowledge of my own future. At that moment, I have no awareness that I am going to spend most of my working life in this, for me, most unlikely of places.

Unlike the refugees in this book, I had made what's called an *economic migration*. I was invited to this country to work because of specialist skills. No traumatic moment swivelled the compass to dictate where I could live my life. In this odd little city that I passed through, opportunities, projects and relationships will just happen to grow like a gossamer web around me until, unexpectedly, it will be more rewarding to stay than to move on.

I sit listening for the first time to the high-pitched otherworldliness of the famous King's College Choir. It's a sound that will punctuate my working days here, marking out several years of blissful immersion in the University's silent, wood-panelled libraries. When they finish, I cross the quadrangle for dinner at High Table, where I am to take my meals. As I go out the Chapel door, a figure in ceremonial garb directs me to walk across the grass because as a Member of High Table I 'have the right to'. He steers everyone else to go the long way round the kerbed edges of the quadrangle. In the Fellows' Lounge, it's dry sherry and hesitating, stilted small-talk before dinner. Then a formal procession in twos walks us ceremonially to High Table to eat. Later, port and snuff travel by us, pushed round the table on a little silver carriage with smooth silver wheels. Apparently you must always push it along from right to left, never the other way. I am relieved to learn the snuff must never stop in front of women. It is for the men.

A dashing young don has been assigned to show me round Cambridge for the evening. He takes me for a drink in a venerable old pub where Nobel scientists have mulled over mathematical dilemmas. Then he announces, flushed: now I'm taking you somewhere *a bit different…!* After the Paris underworld, I'm ready for anything. Does Cambridge have its own *Moulin Rouge* or red-light district? He leads me across town to an ancient lamp-post that stands half-way across a dark green. He points up at a much-renewed piece of old graffiti on it that says:

Reality Checkpoint ➤

The arrow points away from us and the university quarter, towards what he explains is the ethnic, working-class part of town. [13] *'And that's where we're going!'*, he shouts, as if we were on safari, heading out into the Serengeti. On the way, he explains Cambridge's ancient *Town versus Gown* divide. Although we had hung up our academic gowns in the Fellows' Vestibule after dinner and come out in civilian garb, apparently we would always be on the *Gown* side of this division.

That night, standing in a pool of light under the lamp-post in the middle of the dark green, no foresight or intuition - no omen in the sky - told me that I'd still be standing in this strange city twenty years later, that I would have become very interested in its *Town-Gown* divide, and would have created this book about it.

---

[13] For those who know Cambridge, this lamp-post known as *'Reality Checkpoint'* - symbolically dividing the territories of *Town* and *Gown* - is in the middle of Parker's Piece, and the arrow points towards Mill Road.

Chapter 1

Ruth

From a mud hut in the African bushlands

A grilled locust is better than no soup

Proverb from Ruth's country

It's many years later and I'm sitting on the lumpy single bed in Ruth's cramped bedsit, very much on the *Town* side of the *Reality Checkpoint* lamp-post. My clipboard is on my knees, ready to take notes. Ruth is out in the communal corridor boiling a kettle to make me a cup of tea. She comes in and sets the tea before me, delighted, as if it's a beverage fit for a queen.

Ruth looks physically strong and healthy, her black skin glowing. She has a warm, calm manner, a radiant smile and a body-shaking laugh that erupts irrepressibly while she talks. She's about 50 years old, she doesn't know for sure. She lives alone. She has three daily jobs as a cleaner, starting at 4am and finishing around 8pm, with a three-hour gap in the middle.

She speaks English fluently now, without the slightest mistake, having learnt it from scratch since arriving in England two years ago. I can tell Ruth is exceptionally intelligent, though she has no awareness of it, having never been to any kind of school. I've seen her rapidly learn perfect spoken English without books or classes, just by listening to co-workers and practising speaking with them. Having taught a foreign language at university level, I know how difficult even gifted graduates find it to learn languages.

She is now learning to read and write. As part of this project, she asked if I could arrange for her to learn to write her name, maybe even write short notes for colleagues at her cleaning jobs. I organised for her to join a free 'Introduction to Literacy' course where she quickly absorbed all they taught her. She's now reading simple library books, since I showed her how to join the library.

She has asked that her pseudonym for this interview be *Ruth*, after Ruth in the Bible. Back home she had often heard Ruth's story read aloud by the pastor in church. But now she feels she knows in her bones that biblical woman who in her later years had to go a country that was foreign and alien, to labour in the fields there alone.

I reach over to switch on the microphone and a secret shiver runs up my spine. This adventure begins here. This book I want to create about refugees' lives - however it will turn out - starts its journey here, at this moment. Who knows what stories will unfold between its covers? I ask Ruth what she thinks of life in England.

Ruth

Living in heaven

You know many people say that when you die you can go to heaven. Well I tell you, I *have* died and *I am in heaven!* Because life here in Cambridge is heaven and you all don't even realise it, that you are living in heaven! That is why I wanted to tell my story. To help Cambridge people to realise that.

I will tell you why it is heaven here. Because here you *Buy one, Get one free…!* (doubles over with laughter for a long time). Just imagine that. For instance I work as a cleaner. And here in Cambridge if you get a job as a cleaner and you work hard, you can pay your rent and pay for food and clothing and medicines and the bus, and then you can send money home to your family as well to support them! In my country nowadays, no matter how hard or how long you work you cannot pay for these things - there is no way. It is heaven here in Cambridge because everything is so unbelievably *cheap* compared to in my country!

For example, see this nice warm fleece jacket I'm wearing. It was £4.99 at the supermarket and it was *Buy one, Get one free!* It's unbelievable. Brand new. Can you *imagine* it? (laughs and laughs) In my country there is no way nowadays that any sort of worker can afford to buy a jacket like this, even if he works so hard all week long. Here it's just a small part of your salary - *plus you buy one, get one free!* In the supermarket you just walk in, you get some tins of tomatoes for 40p and it's *Buy one, Get one free!* It's unbelievable. It's like they are giving it all away. In my country no-one can afford a tin of tomatoes anymore, no matter how long they work. A tin of tomatoes has become like a dream. So we are all living in heaven here in Cambridge.

Where I come from, the people, they are dying - actually dying every day, lots and lots of them. Here in Cambridge, elderly people have a pension to live on and nice accommodation and all the food and medicine they need. The government gives them all this if they don't have the money themselves. *They even go free on the bus!* (laughing and laughing) But back home where I come from - if you came there with me this minute - you would see our elderly people just lying on the ground inside the door of a hut or a concrete room, just lying on the bare ground with nothing - nothing - just waiting to die. They have no way of getting any food, clothes, medicines, nothing.

And so many of our children are Aids orphans now as well. Every time I phone home I am afraid now to ask about the extended family and the neighbours. I used to ask for news about everyone and say *Oh how is Mr. So-and-so and Mrs. So-and-so?* And my family would say *Didn't you know? Oh, he has died, she has died, they have died.* So now I am almost afraid to ask after our friends and neighbours. For instance, our friend has just died of Aids. He had three wives. Two of them have now died of it as well. In that household there were ten children in all. So now the surviving wife is left alone with all ten small orphans and she just cannot feed them. She is not going to be able to feed them. There is no food anywhere. How can she feed them? This is what I hear when I phone home. So you see what I mean about the tin of tomatoes - it just costs a tiny part of my salary as a cleaner, just like that. Plus they give you another tin for free, for no reason.

So we are living in heaven here in Cambridge. I am so lucky because I work at different cleaning jobs at different times during the day. And sometimes I manage to get some extra cleaning work in the evenings too, after my day of work. It's great. Sometimes people ask me why I don't get tired, doing extra work in the evenings on top. But I don't get tired. I can't get tired. God won't let me get tired. God gives me all the energy I need. Because I have to send money home to feed my children, and the neighbours' children as well, because so many are orphans now. So I am very happy to find extra work any time. I can't get tired (smiling).

My children are in Africa

I want to tell my story because I want people to know how *good* things are here in Cambridge. How lucky they are, and how I thank God for bringing me here. I want them to know about all the good people here who have helped me so much. But I also want them to know something about how things are for other people in other parts of the world like my country, where things are very, very different. And I want to thank God for all the good things that have happened to me to bring me here to be able to work in Cambridge.

But first of all I have to tell you again that I can't say anything about anything political. Nothing at all. You know that there have been lots of political difficulties and violence in my country for a long time. But because of my family I'm not going to discuss that at all with you. Because my family are still there. Also I have asked you to change my name when I tell my story. You can call me Ruth, like the lady in the Bible!

My children are still in Africa, but from here I can support them. That is how my children can stay alive. In our family we have a policy now of not speaking at all about politics. We are Christians, and real Christians cannot take sides and get involved in politics. Even if they come banging on the door in the middle of the night and even if neighbours are very involved, we don't react now. We just work as hard as we can to feed our family and to live as good Christians. Long ago when my husband was with me, he said to me: '*Ruth, we are the poor. And on this earth, the poor can rely only on God.*'

My youngest child back home is only 8 and the older girl is 12. They need me to be here working to support them so they can eat. That is why I am happy and I thank God for being here and for having my cleaning jobs. I am able to talk on the phone to my eight-year-old as often as I can afford to buy a phone card. Recently she asked to be put on the line to me on the phone. She said '*Momma, I want to say a prayer together with you now. I want to thank God that you are able to work there in Cambridge for us. Because that way we can eat. The other children around here, Momma, they cannot eat. But we are OK because of you Momma, and you working there in Cambridge so we can eat. So let's thank God now that you are there, Momma, although I miss you.*' But I said '*OK, that's enough now*' and I got off the line because I didn't want to hear anymore about her friends who cannot eat.

I grew up with my grandma, which was common in my country then. She was a really wonderful woman - a very special person. She raised me and I worked alongside her growing all our food and everything we needed in our garden. That was our life and we were very happy. The only thing we bought with money at the market was soap. Grandma grew all her own maize and we ground down the corn by hand to make *mealy-meal*, our main food. I think it's called 'polenta' here. It only takes about 15 minutes to cook in water, like porridge. Then you fluff it up with a fork like mashed potato. It's really nice. We were never, ever, short of it while grandma grew it for us, and our life was good.

I still believe it's very important to not just go out and look to buy your food at the market. That is not the way to do it. Look at my grandma and what she was able to produce on her own little patch of ground, just by being clever and working hard. So no - you should not go looking about everywhere trying to find some mealy-meal to buy somewhere. Then you totally depend on whether you can find any, and whether you have enough money for it. No - *you must grow it yourself*, that's all! I really think it is the only way.

You must get the seeds and store them up and then prepare the ground at the right time of year and do the work each day, each week, all the year, to tend your plants. Then you will have your own maize-crop. Then after you harvest it you can grind all the maize yourself by hand and store it. That way your family will eat even when no-one else has any money to buy any food.

It's the same with cooking oil. I see now that back home everyone is trying so hard to be able to find a bit of cooking-oil to buy at the market. No. You should start at the beginning and plant ground-nuts (you call them peanuts here in England). Then you can grow your ground-nut crop during the year. Then when you harvest it, you can grind the ground-nuts down by hand and produce your own cooking-oil. You store that in the house and your family are OK for cooking-oil till the next year, even if there is no money anywhere and no-one can buy cooking-oil at the market. My grandma taught me how to do all these things, and it really works.

But I notice that hardly any other family besides ours now grows their own mealy-meal or cooking-oil. Maybe it is hard work, but I notice that since all the war and violence, the people now have got so discouraged and tired, and maybe lazy. So many people are sick with HIV and Aids and there are so, so many orphans. And many people have just lost the knowledge as well - as well as the will - to know how to grow their food on their own bit of ground like we did, and like my family still do.

Teaching self-sufficiency

So with my children, what I do now over the phone from Cambridge is I direct them every week when I phone, telling them exactly how to produce the crops in our garden. Every week I tell them exactly what to do that week and they must do it. I can see all the garden in my head, and I can recall the things that need doing in each week of the year. So I guide and direct them from here and they do it over there! I say *'This week you must pick those two rows of onions on the far right side at the back, and store them carefully in the house. You must not eat the two rows of beans yet - wait till I tell you. And this week you must plant two rows of tomatoes over on the left side, where you've taken out the maize harvest. And above all the most important thing is that for each crop, you must choose the very best quality of each and not eat that one. That one you must store as seed for next year's planting, so you will have a good quality crop again next year.'*

It is very important not to just eat your best seed this year! Things like that - like how to rotate the crops in each row and the exact time to plant and pick them - I am able to direct them in all that from here. So I am very happy because I can imagine them sitting down together and eating these crops they have grown, and then I know they will be alright. This is knowledge and training that I can give my children even from here, when I am not with them, and this alone makes the difference that they can eat when others cannot.

But I believe that it's not just about practical knowledge. I think the most important thing is to train a young person up so that inside they know that whatever happens, whatever country they're in, whether they're with their family or out on their own - they can always, always pick themselves up and go out and find some work to do so that someone will pay them a little for doing it. And then they can buy some seed and build up a little corner where they can produce their own bit of food by their own work, and they can be OK.

I believe it is possible to do that little bit anywhere, any time. I believe that if you make that effort and work hard, then God will always help you. He will give you the energy you need. You don't just give up, or give in to feeling tired or hungry or sick, or give up because of the political problems or the war in your country. There is always a way to find a little work to get started, and then to plant your own little corner of food and grow it, and save some seed so you can grow even more next year.

That is what I really believe. I believe it's actually the same whether you are well-off in Cambridge or hungry in my country. In either situation, many people give up and sink down and find reason to complain. Here in Cambridge for instance I have to say if I'm honest that I see a lot of people living on benefits - sickness benefits - when they look perfectly healthy to me. I observe these people very closely and I can't see anything wrong with their bodies. I've been thinking about it a lot trying to figure it out and I thought maybe it's that they all just have mental illnesses in their heads that I can't see, that only a specialist doctor can see (smiles and laughs).

But I do see that they're well enough to go about all day, going to town on the bus and buying their food and going to the cinema and walking and feeding their dog. And I think someone who can do all that is well enough to do some bit of useful work too really if they wanted to. So there's some things like that that I don't fully understand about life in Cambridge - why the government gives them so much benefit when they could be working a little. If only they had the desire inside them to do something and look ahead and be a bit active to make a better life for their family... That is how my grandma raised me and I believe that's how all true Christians have to be.

When you are a true Christian, you accept everybody and you say nothing negative to anyone ever. But inside yourself you are always looking for ways to look ahead, to plan your life, and to do little things now that would build up a better life for your family. Isn't that the right way way to live, whether you are rich or poor? The other thing a true Christian does is when there are problems with others - with a husband or neighbours or with people you work with - you try to fix the problem with sweetness, not with more harsh words because that will never work. True sweetness is the only thing that works with human beings, I find.

What to do about 'racism'

Sometimes Black friends here come to me and say: *'Oh Ruth, such-and-such a White person is being racist to me. They are racist. They don't like me because I am Black and they're against me...'* And do you know what I say to that friend? I say: *'Honey, it's all in your own head!'*

I have thought about this a lot and I believe that if you think there is 'racism' against you, then in one way it is really coming from you - from your own head - isn't it? Isn't it you who are using the word 'racist' and worrying about what may or may not be going on in someone else's head? So I say to my friend *'What does she care about you, that White woman? And why are you trying to mind that man's business? You cannot truly know what is going on inside that woman's head. So you imagine she is thinking all about you, that she's thinking "That Black woman - I don't like Black people, I won't talk to her, I won't sit next to that Black woman on the bus, I won't be nice to her at work...'*

So you convince yourself that you feel sure that's what she's thinking. But you're the crazy one! Because she's not even thinking about you, sweetie! Deep down she's thinking about her own life. Her head is full of her own worries and she's thinking about her own family and about doing her own job. Where do you think she's going to get the time to be also thinking about you on top of all that?! Huh? Seriously?! (laughs and laughs)

So do you know where the 'racism' is coming out of? It's coming out of your own head. You're just nervous about that idea of 'racism' in your own head so if it happens that some White woman doesn't talk to you at work one day, you think 'Oh she's racist, she doesn't like Black people.' Or if someone sits in another seat on the bus instead of sitting down next to you, you think 'There it is - more racism!' (laughs a lot).

But this is crazy. And it's dangerous, because of course it can build up and up in your head and then it's very difficult to stop it and get back out of it. You should never let this start in your head like a little seed, because it could grow and grow. A true Christian could never think like that, that other people were 'racist'. If you're a Christian, inside you're always just thinking *'God loves me, and I like everyone else too'* and you just get on with your own life cheerfully. That's it - nothing else.

I'm busy all the time thinking ahead about my life and my work and my family. How could I have time for sitting around thinking I don't like someone, or imagining whether they are 'racist'? That sort of thing comes out of your own head, and it is yourself who should stop it in your head. Forget about whatever you think the other guy may be doing in his head - it's not your problem.

Learning to read

I can tell you that the one thing I found hardest when I came here to Cambridge was to learn English. It has taken me two whole years to learn your language. I started each day with one word and then another word and trying to put them together and that is the way I learned. I am so happy that I can speak with you now in your own language. But there was one more thing that I wanted to achieve yet. It was like a little dream for me.

I dreamed that I could find a way to learn a small bit of reading and writing. Just enough to be able to write a note at work if I needed to leave a note for my boss. Or to leave a note for a friend if I'm going to be late for an appointment with her. That would make me so happy, to be able to do that. I was thinking a lot about how I could learn that. I felt I could learn it in a quick time. Then you arranged the classes for me and it was really great. They taught me so well and it was really not so hard at all. I'm reading easy library books now as well. It has really completed my feeling that I am making the most of my time while I am here in Cambridge.

When I leave Cambridge in the future, I will know now that my story and the story of the people like me in the world has been told in this book. That will make me very happy and my family will be proud. It has been an amazing experience for me to come and live and work here. I have had this chance to come and see and learn so many new things in this bigger world, this world you all live in here.

And I wanted to tell people my story so that they can step out of their little world for a moment too, like I stepped out of my world back home. And maybe through my story, they can see a bit of what the world is like for other people far away from Cambridge, like in my country. That is what I would like. And I thank God for bringing me to such a beautiful place and to such good, kind people who have done nothing but help me in so many ways.

 Sitting on my own bed back at home, I review my clip-board of notes and think about Ruth's interview. Economics, leadership, linguistic gifts, self-sufficiency, ways to get around depending on capitalist markets... These are the deeply unlikely topics raised by this illiterate woman displaced from the African bush into a sophisticated western city.

Her description of how 'cheap' everything is in Cambridge, too, is the last thing in the world I would have expected her to say. Cambridge is the second most expensive city of the UK, and we all complain about it. To her it all seems incredibly affordable compared to the unattainability of food, clothing and housing in her starving shanty-town.

I am awed by this person's resilience, resourcefulness, positivity, ethics and appetite for work. I've already seen that most of the refugees I'll be interviewing seem to have these traits. Is it that individuals with those qualities are more likely to resist corrupt regimes back home, and hence end up needing political asylum? Or are more likely to try to escape and build a new life from nothing elsewhere rather than 'give up', as Ruth put it?

Circumstances have left her the role of long-distance leader for an extended clan network of mostly young and elderly dependents. But she's like a living catalogue of the behaviours required for success in life. You'd think she'd been coached by a personal development life-coach. How to earn, save, manage money and avoid being over-dependent on things sold by others. How to secure the resources to stay alive, how to manage one's thoughts. She reframes 'racism' as existing only in the victim's mind, which empowers the victim to control it by controlling their own reaction to it.

Seeing Ruth's inner mastery of life-skills, it makes me wonder how well African countries could thrive if their famously resourceful people weren't held back by corrupt leadership. I have seen regular letters from the head-master of her daughters' school back home, extorting corrupt fees and extra payments from her. She needed a simple photocopy of her daughter's birth certificate, which he had in his office, and he charged her £110 sterling for the photocopy, a sum I saw her wire off to him at the post-office.

I realise that hearing my interviewees' stories is going to be a way of travelling without going anywhere. I wonder where tomorrow's interview will take me. All I know is that the journey will start on the choppy waves of the South China Sea...

Chapter 2

Hanh

From the Vietnamese *'Boat People'*

A frog living at the bottom of a well
thinks the sky is as small as the lid of a cooking-pot

Vietnamese saying

 Hanh is a small woman in her forties. She has a strong, compact body and a lively, intelligent face. She speaks rapidly, with energy, and seems a woman who takes no nonsense. Her extended family own two Chinese takeaways in the most ethnic part of town (where the 'Reality' sign on the lamp-post points to).

As a nine-year-old, Hanh was one of thousands of 'Boat People' who had to leave everything and crowd onto small fishing-boats to escape onto the treacherous waters of the South China Sea, fleeing the war that had broken out around them between China and Vietnam.

In Hanh's case, 64 people crowded onto one little twenty-foot boat, thinking they'd be on it briefly. Unbelievably, they spent three months out at sea on that boat, unable to dock anywhere.

How on earth did the tiny nine-year-old make it to Cambridge?

Hanh

War

Yes, we were on that tiny boat for three months, so it was quite an experience...! People say, 'Oh, you're a *Boat Person?*' But it is nothing to be ashamed of. [14]

My family is ethnic Chinese but we'd always lived in North Vietnam, quite near the Chinese border. It was a big town, about the size of Cambridge. I remember the sea in front of our house and a lake, plus a river and mountains behind. We had a massive garden, with the kitchen and the toilets built separately in the gardens. We kept chickens and a couple of pigs and my mum grew our vegetables. My dad was a builder and he did pretty well. There were six of us children, two boys and four girls. We would spend our time swimming and fishing. In those days - this was the late seventies - there was no danger. As a kid you were free to go where you wanted. From when I was about eight, I used to babysit for a neighbour as well - not for money or anything, just to help out.

I remember that my mum was always really hard working. She'd get up at 2am some mornings to go over the river to China to buy things that we couldn't get in Vietnam - Chinese foods like dried squid. She would come back with all this stuff strapped to her! If the border police caught her, my mum would have to bribe them or they'd confiscate all her stuff. It could get expensive. Once she even carried back live fish without them noticing. I don't know how she managed it!

I suppose growing up I knew that being ethnic Chinese in Vietnam, we were different as a family but it wasn't a big deal. We spoke Cantonese at home and learned Vietnamese at school, but I've completely forgotten the Vietnamese language now. At school there were about ten other Chinese in my class. Ethnic Chinese people like us stood out in Vietnam because our

---

[14] A version of this interview appeared in the community magazine *Cambridge Untold*.

skin is lighter. But I had always thought of Vietnam as my home - for a child, where you live is home. So when war suddenly broke out between China and Vietnam in 1979 and people started calling us names, it was really weird.

They started saying 'Go back to your country!' But for me Vietnam *was* my country! I think people were also a bit jealous of us ethnic Chinese, because we're really hard working and so we're usually richer. The police got really unpleasant too. There was nothing like human rights, or anything like that. And I remember my dad telling us all that we would have to run away now from Vietnam. Suddenly we didn't belong.

The journey of the *'Boat People'*

What happened was that my 18-year old brother and I were sent over the border into China to my uncle's, to arrange a place for the whole family to join us. After a few weeks they all had to flee from Vietnam too. The government was throwing all Chinese people out. It would have been dangerous to stay. We had to just leave everything - our house, all our possessions. Although I didn't have any toys to leave behind anyway, not even dolls. It wasn't that we were poor, just that there weren't any toys in Vietnam at that time.

I remember that my dad had saved a case of Vietnamese bank notes, and that was supposed to last us a while. But they devalued the currency and overnight all our savings became worthless! So all we had was a few clothes and our passports. I was devastated about leaving my friends. Our next-door neighbours were Vietnamese, but they were always nice to us. They actually wanted to escape the Communist government too, but there were too many of them to leave.

Once we had fled to the Chinese side, one of my uncles bought this boat and said that we should all leave in it and go to Hong Kong. It was still British in those days and they would take us in. That's if we made it on the long trip over the South China Sea. I heard the adults talking about storms and shark-infested waters and pirate raids....

I was shocked when I saw the boat: it was only about 20 feet long. It was designed for five people, but my uncle took other people for a fare. In the end we set off with 64 of us squashed into it! It had a sail and an engine. My dad had worked as a fisherman and so he was going to be the captain.

The first thing to do was to get enough food on board to last for the journey. My dad bought a lot of belly of pork and us kids salted it so it wouldn't go off. Salted pork, salted fish and dry biscuits was all we had to eat on the journey. Horrible! We cooked with a gas bottle at one end of the boat where all the food was stored. You can imagine how cramped it was! There was nowhere to lie down - we all had to sit all the time on benches. At night we curled up on them against each other. Of course people got on each others' nerves. I will never forget: there was this seven-months pregnant woman beside me. I hated her! She was seasick and kept throwing up all over me! She took up a lot of room and made my life hell! She was actually a single mother, a group of people who were looked down on in China in those days.

My mum was so worried about my little one-and-a-half-year-old sister. My older brother was really good - he helped my dad out. Our family sat together and held hands a lot. When it rained we pulled a tarpaulin over us and sat there miserably waiting for it to stop. We sat upright on that tiny boat for three months.

My dad was a good sailor. He was always looking at the sky for storms. We sat there at night on our crowded benches holding hands and praying for no storms! We did actually have a storm and luckily for us, my dad put into an island in time. I remember this boy got a snake-bite on the island and I thought 'Oh, no, he's going to die'. But my dad found these plants to treat him with. My dad was the captain, the doctor, everything... He's 74 now and is out cooking till midnight every night at our takeaway. He loves it!

My other uncle, my mum's brother, captained a larger boat with about 160 passengers, behind us. My uncle thought he could make it through the storm but his boat got caught in a whirlpool. The boat got smashed up and they were pulled under. Only three people survived - my uncle, his step-daughter and one other passenger. My uncle lost his wife, children, everyone. In Vietnam he had been really wealthy selling jewellery, with two wives and a massive house with servants... Now he was left with nothing and no-one.

Once, I remember we signalled to a big Chinese ship. We were waving and flashing lights. We begged them to tow us some of the way. Our money was useless, so they asked for gold. My mum and my aunty and everybody else had to hand over their rings and earrings. Eventually we got towed to Hong Kong harbour where the harbour police put us on a really big ship. We were so relieved! I remember my dad saying there had been five other boats behind us, but only two had made it. I knew what happened to those poor people. Storms, sharks, pirates. That could have been us...

Life in a refugee camp

I didn't like the Hong Kong police much. I think they'd had droves of Boat People constantly arriving and they were sick of the sight of us! In Hong Kong they put us in a camp which was like a massive hangar for storing goods, not people. Our family were in a room about 12 foot square - no bed or anything. We slept on the floor. Every morning we got only two slices of bread with sweetened condensed milk on it. *Carnation*, I remember the brand. Now I can't touch condensed milk! Ugh! It reminds me too much.

At night there were these large rats running around. It was awful. My dad as the head of the family had to go and queue up for food, bringing it back and sharing it out. It was never enough. My poor mum wasn't producing any milk for my baby sister so we always saved her an extra piece of bread. I remember some people traded their gold ring for a pack of cigarettes!

After a couple of weeks we were moved to a more permanent camp. That was better because they gave us ID cards and we had to go and find jobs. My dad and my older brother and sister got jobs - cleaning, working in factories, that sort of thing. I did all the shopping, aged nine, because my mum was not very well. In the end I earned some money looking after people's kids while they went out to work. In the camp there was no privacy, we all slept in rows and rows of bunk beds. That lasted a year. I was terrified as a kid having to share with all these people because you really didn't know who they were. Some girls got raped. I remember my dad used to stay awake at night to keep watch over us.

There was one guy who slept in the bunk opposite us. One night he was in a deep sleep because he had been working so hard. Well, these Vietnamese boys, three of them, turned up and stabbed him to death as he slept right there in front of us. My dad saw it all. He called the police but they did not do a thing. It had a real effect on me and my sister. I could not sleep after that. I will never forget the blood dripping from the murdered boy's top bunk onto the woman who was on the bunk below. Who knows why they murdered him? A row about a girl, some said.

In fact a lot of people got killed in that camp. Can you believe it? People killing each other after they had just fled the Communist take-over and spent months at sea in crowded boats and just escaped with their lives?

Sometimes I try not to remember all this. If you hadn't asked me I wouldn't choose to remember it. In fact, in our big extended family now, we never talk about it. It's all in the past - we look to the future. Sometimes it will crop up, but more to remind the younger members that they should be grateful that they are alive and lucky enough to be living in Britain. That they should not waste their lives or their money gambling, for example.

Coming to Cambridge

By the time we got asylum in England I was twelve. My dad chose England and not America because he said they have too many guns and too much shooting in America. He said in England people were nice and everyone rode around on bikes - it would be lovely! That was before we ever thought about Cambridge. But as the plane touched down at Heathrow, to me England looked dark and miserable. We were taken to a reception centre in Watton near Norwich. All the way, I remember my mum looking miserably out of the window of the minibus at the dark motorway. She had heard they would feed us only potatoes! But when we got to the centre we were given our own little house and they had cooked chicken and fish... *and rice!* I have never seen my mum look so relieved and happy!

Although I don't go around thinking *'I was a Boat-Person'*, it does affect how I live. Sometimes I'll catch myself looking at my small daughter and think: 'You are *so-oo* lucky'. Or she'll say 'Buy me this, Mummy' and I say 'Sweetheart, when Mummy was your age, she didn't have all these things...' And she'll go 'Why?' and I will tell her a little bit about how Grandma and Grandad and all her uncles and aunties had to escape in a boat.

My sister-in-law fled Vietnam on another boat. Now she runs our two takeaway businesses here in Cambridge. She went back a few years ago to visit our village in Vietnam but after twenty-eight years, she couldn't recognise it. They had built a block of flats where her house stood. She hasn't told her children about the boat journey or about the refugee camp in Hong Kong. She says she's too busy, and that they have their lives to live. One is studying IT at university, another is studying design in London.

My nephew mans our takeaway most nights. He was born right across the road. He says 'My family came all the way from Vietnam, but I've only had to come across the road!' Until now he had never heard all these amazing stories from his aunties or grandparents. Everyone in our family is too busy working. I guess it's our Chinese work ethic. He says we work too hard!

 That evening, with the notes from Hanh's interview strewn around me, I watch open-mouthed as TV reports show that - all these years later - almost a thousand present-day *Boat People* have just drowned in the Mediterranean off Italy. We used to think *Boat People* were a thing of the past, but it's clear they're a thing of the future. And today's are much more numerous than the *Boat People* of the 80s were, and much closer to us geographically. And they're not streaming from just one temporary, local conflict, but from multiple conflict-zones.

Economic migrants choose to leave home for a better place but Hanh's people had their sense of being 'at home' ripped away before they ever left. They were driven out because one morning they woke up on the wrong side of an ethnic divide that had suddenly flashed up around them. I am wondering what 'wrong sides' my next interviewees will have found themselves on, forcing them to flee.

In Hanh's people, the appetite for work is clearly huge, as it was in Ruth in the first chapter. For Hanh's elderly father, work is a joy - he 'loves it'. He's working by choice, in a self-employed business with loved ones, having 'made it' across the perilous seas that he guided them over. Ruth, on the other hand, doesn't claim to 'love' her cleaning-work. She just does as much of it as humanly possible because it helps her loved ones who are still in chaos back home. But for Hanh's people, you sense that work has been the forward motor: a focus for their healing, a distraction, an anchor, a means of forgetting, a way of building a new life.

Hanh's father and Ruth have both shown that exceptional resourcefulness that made them a leader in a crisis - literally a life-saver for their extended group. He took skills he already had from his old lifestyle, sailing small boats as a fisherman, and transferred them to the disaster at hand, successfully navigating 64 people over the high seas in a little overloaded boat for months on end. Ruth took what she had learned on grandma's veg-patch, drew it up into an elaborate visualisation that evolves across the seasons, and now dictates horticultural tasks long-distance over the phone, thus protecting her little clan from the starvation that surrounds them.

I can see that memory is going to be a big theme in this book - and the dilemmas of what to do with memories. Some of the people I'm going to interview have said they want their memories recorded in detail. Others forewarned me that they'll have to skip over whole areas and not discuss them at all. Hanh seemed ambivalent. On the one hand her people 'look to the future' and her sister-in-law has never told her children the horrors of their migration. Hanh herself feels shaken when recounting the violent deaths she witnessed first-hand as a child refugee. But when her Cambridge five-year-old demands treats, Hanh thinks it's salutary to outline for her the deprivations that the previous generations survived.

Chapter 3

Talya

From an occupied territory in the Middle East

Freedom is never given, but taken

Saying from Talya's culture

 The tiny studio flat feels dim and shrouded. There are full-length windows that could look out on a pretty green space outside, but long curtains are pulled shut over them. A television is on in the background. I get the sense it's on permanently for some kind of desperate reason - for company and background distraction, to fill the darkened silence a bit.

The young woman has pale, blue-green eyes and a soft, expressive, heart-shaped face. Her skin is pallid. She has long, thick, wavy, black hair, with a few premature grey strands.

She's polite and welcoming but when we get talking I can see she's suffering from an agitated anxiety, and some sort of chronic depression. I get the sense that's probably not her original character. Later, as she talks on, I see flashes of a fiery, romantic woman behind the shroud of agitated paralysis. And I can guess at the dynamic young lawyer she used to be.

The one ray of light in the dim room is the four-month old baby she clearly adores. I note with relief that she has natural mothering skills and that despite her own despair, the baby is expertly cared-for. She shines her attention and intelligence onto him like a bright light every few minutes, playing with him, talking to him, picking him up to exercise him cheerfully on her knees.

I am amazed to see that at one point the four-month-old pretty much 'stands' on her lap! He stiffens his legs rigid - just long enough to support his own weight for a moment. She supports him just enough to stop him tipping sideways, but he seemed to hold his own weight for a moment before buckling again under the effort. She laughs and congratulates him warmly and he looks very proud indeed. They both sink back down delighted and he retires to lie in his pram again for a while. I ask her 'Is that normal - that he can nearly stand at only four months?' She beams - a mixture of pride and modesty, as if acknowledging that she's training up a champion. She laughs and says, 'I train him a lot!'

I ask her how she came to be here.

Talya

I was a lawyer for political prisoners back home. Here is the official report about me from the Medical Foundation for Victims of Torture in London. It tells how I came here, if you want to see it - it includes my whole story. They helped me a lot when I first arrived here. I can give you the report. I came here really because I just wanted to live - to stay alive, stay out of prison. It hasn't been easy for me of course because I am a human and I need lots of things. In the past I had lots of good things and I had to leave them all. My friends, my house, my family, a good job, a career, my country, my language… That was all very important to me, but I had to leave it all behind and go with nothing, to stay alive.

After that, I needed to learn the language because when I came here I didn't speak any English at all, although I knew the German language. Those might seem like small things, but it's not been easy. Every day is such a big change. I haven't got a job now and that's so difficult for me as I was used to having a busy career in the law courts. Sometimes I feel really tired. Sometimes I forget who I am. Lots of things are so different. Sometimes I feel like a child, trying to learn how to live all over again.

My husband is also a refugee, but he has to live in a different European country. He was a political prisoner in our country for seven years, for purely political reasons. He was able to get asylum in another west European country soon after I came here. He will eventually become a citizen there. I want to become a British citizen, of course, but I need to stay here for at least five years before that can start. I want to go on to do a Master's degree in human rights law. After that I want to work in Africa or similar countries. I would really like to do that kind of work. I searched a bit for a university. Essex University does that degree, and Oxford too, but it's so expensive.

I come from a politically active family. My eldest brother was stabbed in our town in 1978 by a right-wing militant. Although I was only about six years old, I clearly remember how he came home covered in blood. One of my cousins was imprisoned for one and a half years after a military coup - for possessing in his bookshop publications that the coup had banned. He was a supporter of a left-wing party. After his release he fled to Austria.

My family's home was raided by the military police twice after the coup. My relatives were left-wing trade union members, and they were all detained on a number of occasions. Their longest detention was for eighteen days in April 1980. With this family background I was already well aware of the political situation in my country as a child, even before I started university.

I studied law at university, and became a member of the student union. I met students from different political groups, including the revolutionary left-wing groups. My brother was also a sympathiser of theirs. Although he never tried to influence my political opinion, I began to sympathise with the movement and became more active with them. I attended their meetings and helped prepare and distribute leaflets for the group. The Communist Party appealed to me because they supported the class struggle to change the regime to benefit working people, instead of just supporting guerrilla activities like many of those resistance groups did. They didn't support armed struggle either at that time, until the revolution started later.

I myself was detained several times. The longest detention was a horrible experience. Myself and my partner were being searched by the police because of our political activities. My house was sealed off during our absence. After hiding for some time we took advice from our solicitors and decided to face the charges. The prosecutor then handed us over to the police. We were brought to a station of the 'anti-terrorist' police branch and detained there for 11 days. My cell there was very small and dark. They did horrible things to us that I will never be able to forget for the rest of my life. I don't want to talk about that here.

After my release I stayed with my sister for a couple of weeks because I was not capable of looking after myself, I was so damaged by those experiences in police custody. My sister helped me a lot during that time. She was also a student, but not politically active.

I was detained once more, after attending the funeral of a revolutionary left supporter who had been killed by the police. Although I was not a supporter, as a rights lawyer I strongly opposed these extra-judicial executions by the police - that was the reason why I attended the funeral. The police arrested about twenty people along with me. I was detained only for a half a day that time, but I was brought to the same police station as before and that brought back all the bad memories.

We were lined up in a corridor and told to write a full report for the police. I refused to do that, but I could see that all but one other person wrote dutifully. That incident made me realise that I could not even trust my activist friends. We were all on our own and at the mercy of the police officers. Instead of defying them collectively, everyone had tried to save their own necks.

As a lawyer I represented both criminal and political cases. I took the criminal ones to earn my living and the political ones for job satisfaction. I charged my political clients very little, usually only the court expenses. I had to visit many of my political activist clients who were on hunger strike in prison. Some of them died during these hunger strikes. Once an activist client died of hunger strike the day after I had visited him in prison. Myself and another solicitor had to go to the morgue to identify his corpse. The autopsy said he had died of 'natural causes', even though he was very young. I remember that his death in prison really upset me.

Some of my political prisoner clients were on hunger strike for very long periods. I personally was against this because I think it is self-destructive and didn't achieve anything to improve the prison conditions. I actually applied for the release of one of my clients despite his protests, so that he could be treated medically. He was released and then immediately hospitalised. I visited him often during his treatment, and even stayed in the hospital with him as a carer.

But I still have to admit that I dreaded the visits to the prisoners on hunger strike. I saw them dying slowly, shrinking to no more than skin and bones. Each time I went in there I thought it was the last time I would see them. I would put on a brave face and tried hard to cheer them up, but I always felt totally depleted when leaving the prison. After leaving the prison I would often sit down on the pavement and just cry. As a solicitor I was also present during the hand-over of the dead bodies of hunger strikers to their families. I tried to console them, but I myself always felt so helpless.

Those visits to the prisons were especially painful for me. Lawyers of political prisoners received a cold reception from the prison officers and sometimes we were openly called 'lawyers of terrorists'. I got used to being thoroughly searched on the way in and out. They would often try to humiliate us that way in front of everyone.

There were several demonstrations organised by human rights groups that were interrupted by the police as 'illegal demonstrations'. I took part in preparing numerous legal complaints to the public prosecutor, but I don't remember any of these applications getting a successful result.

At that time I joined a group of solicitors from the Contemporary Lawyers Association who wanted to give a press conference. They were protesting against proposed new legislation that would restrict solicitors' access to their clients. The chair of the association at the time attempted to talk to the media. The police immediately intervened and arrested the solicitors - about 50 solicitors! I was among these people who were detained once again.

After a notorious incident in one of the prisons, I went to visit some of the women prisoners who had been burned during this incident. I did not represent any of those women but the other solicitors and I went there to see if we could assist them in any way. They all needed medical attention, which involved writing countless letters to different authorities, very often without any result. Getting a special diet for a diabetic inmate, for example, could take many months due to the prison bureaucracy. But we wouldn't give up easily.

Only a few days later, I went to a prison to visit a client, but on that occasion I was suddenly not allowed to leave because of my past record. I was told that I was still wanted by the police in relation to the incidents years back, although I had already been acquitted as not guilty back then. They kept me there for six hours and told me they could imprison me whenever they wanted.

I often represented under-age minors at court. There was a system for unaccompanied minors and I was often assigned as their lawyer. I also sometimes had them stay at my place until their families could be found.

Once I was called in for a young man of gypsy origin. When I arrived at the police station they told me that the young man did not want a lawyer. I could not believe that and insisted on hearing it from him myself. After an argument they finally agreed and brought him downstairs. He told me he did want a lawyer, but within a minute he was ushered away to another room. The officers still insisted he did not want my assistance. I made an official complaint about these police officers, but the case was still pending when I had to leave the country.

I met my future husband while visiting a client in prison. After I had talked to my client I found out that the inmates were blockading the doors in a certain part of the prison as a protest. This happened very often in those days. I spoke with them and it was there that I met a few inmates from the Communist party, and he was among them. I only got to really meet him after his release a few years later. When we started dating he reminded me of this incident, when we had met that day in the prison.

He was held for seven years as a political prisoner and after his release he also, like me, fled from the country. As I mentioned, he got asylum in a western European country where he is living today, and we were able to marry even though we have to live in different countries. We rarely get to see each other. Back home, despite staying in prison for seven and a half years, he is still a wanted man. His house was regularly raided even after his release and sometimes he had to hide at my place.

Lots of times I feel irritated and lonely in this country now. That's normal - it's not other peoples' responsibility. Of course, I've met lots of good people here. For example, at the Medical Foundation for Victims of Torture in London, where I was sent first, they really helped me. They really encouraged me so much. I started painting there. But when I came here to this flat I couldn't paint anymore. I don't have enough space.

But I do have a lot of contact with my family back home. We phone each other and I contact them via the internet - that way the calls are very cheap. My parents haven't got internet, but my sisters and brothers and a good friend have.

And I have a small baby now. He was born here, because my husband was able to come to see me here a few times for short visits from his asylum-country. But we don't know when he'll be able to visit us again here.

There is a club here in Cambridge for young women to meet, bringing their babies, so I try to go there sometimes with my baby. He usually doesn't sleep much at night so in the day-time, I'm really, really tired. Mostly I just stay here alone with him all day in this dark little room. I know it's not good for me. Every week I go to a medical clinic where they check up on me and on the baby.

Before I had the baby I used to go out here in Cambridge. I often went to the city-centre and I used to read a lot of books in my language. I also borrowed some easy English books, easy enough for my level. Before having the baby I read a lot in English about pregnancy, about having babies, and I understood those books. But, of course, I don't fully understand books about law and those things yet in English - they're too difficult. I try to watch television, too, to improve my English, and I still go to the library sometimes.

 A few days later I sit in my office reading over the transcript of Talya's interview. Beside it is a copy of the report she gave me about her from the Medical

Foundation for the Victims of Torture, who treated her when she first arrived in this country. Being a solicitor, she was keen for me to have it. For her, official documents that are certified truthful by law have an intrinsic value, even when all else is chaos.

Talya was generous with the details of her memories. In the world of a solicitor, verifiable facts can and must be recorded, and acted upon. For lawyers, there is such a thing as *truth*. She clearly felt too that her testimony was the only vehicle for the truths of so many other people. The stories of those she had to leave behind in those prisons, and those she saw die there, would never be told if she didn't try to tell them.

It had been Talya's whole vocation - her trained profession - to get to the truths of others and have those truths witnessed and recorded in the safe environment of a court of law. But in her efforts to do that she lost her own world - lost everything except her biological survival. She lost her home, family, friends, career, country, language, health, confidence and ability to work.

Putting the papers down, my thoughts go to her husband. I saw that man with her once from a distance, in a crowded café that's frequented by their compatriots in Cambridge. I didn't know who he was then or what his story was. But I remember being struck - as if in a dream or in slow-motion - by that stranger's eyes in the crowd. With his tired, unshaven, rather crumpled face, he looked like all the other men around him. Except for his eyes. I thought so much afterwards about those eyes.

His eyes were an even paler blue-green than Talya's: a sparkling, underwater, crystal blue. They seemed to see farther, deeper, sharper than other eyes do. Eyes that have dreamed, or looked upon other worlds. When I heard later that that man had been a political prisoner for seven years, I could not square that idea with those eyes. I couldn't fit those eyes into the narrative of a person who had been made to spend seven years looking at a wall, just for aspiring for the freedom of his people.

I could not imagine those eyes locked up. In that noisy cafe, in his tired, unshaven face, those unforgettable blue eyes just didn't *look* like they had ever been locked up.

With Talya, a theme I'm seeing for the first time - and surely it will come again in other interviews - is mental health that's been damaged by the experiences that caused the refugee to flee, and by the refugee experience itself. Ruth and Hanh were in rude good health but Talya is agitated and distressed by loops of trauma that play over and over inside her head. As a child Hanh had witnessed violent deaths right in front of her. But she felt protected through those life-and-death moments by her father, at her side defending his little brood as best he could. In Talya's prison-cell, there was no-one to stand between her and her torturers. No-one to even attempt to defend her - she who had been others' defence-lawyer. The deeper damage from that experience was still working its way through the levels of the young woman's brain years later, as she sat alone every day in her cell-like room in Cambridge, the curtains drawn.

I wipe away a hot little tear of gratitude that has spilled onto my papers. I feel gratitude towards this and any country that takes in people like Talya, and towards the other European country for taking in her husband. I've often despised England for its brutal colonial history. But that was then, and right now this country decided to rescue Talya - to just get her out of there, away from her own nation who were destroying her, and to give her a new life in safety here in England. She couldn't speak a word of English at that point. She had nothing to offer. She would need lots of help and support. But they just decided to do it - just for the humanity of it, for no gain. I felt proud, that we have countries around the world who will do these things now, whatever harms they themselves might have done in the past.

I was really rooting for Talya. I believed she would recover. She felt bleak and incapable now but she had generous, careful medical support. The English state was housing her and supporting her. She was in touch with good compatriots here in the city. She had her natural intelligence and her political energies, still burning away like embers under the ashes of her situation. She had the baby with the strong legs. And somewhere, sitting in his own asylum in a little room across the North Sea, she had the man with those eyes.

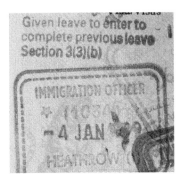

Chapter 4

Samir

From a manor estate in Africa

No one likes to eat crumbs from a feast - everyone likes to sit at the table

Saying from Samir's country

Glancing over my notes before going to meet Samir, I stop short at the sight of the address. He has found a flat in one of Cambridge's many new building developments, after a long and painful search in this city of scarce, expensive accommodation. *Ruth Bagnall Court*, the address says. He won't know it, but I used to know someone who now lives on in that place-name.

She was a very tall young woman. Elegant in an idiosyncratic, gangly sort of way. Vivacious, animated, unusual. She was the leader of the City Council, an elected politician whose portfolio in the city was housing. I only knew her to nod to, but had often heard her famously eloquent speeches in the city parliament about the need for more social housing and better housing for the poor. In her day-job she was a gifted linguist and translator associated with the University.

When I was dating my husband, she sat nearby once on a date of her own. It was in a wood-panelled rowing pub called The Cambridge Blue. I remember watching her idly as she chatted happily to the man. I thought she was what in France we used to call *charmante* - that she had a personal charm unique to herself as a woman, a certain *je ne sais quoi*. A few months later I heard she was gone, plucked away by a lightning cancer.

And now, though she is gone, her name is grafted onto a new-built place - the smart, attractive flat-blocks of *Ruth Bagnall Court*. Samir's wife opens the door to me. She is a tiny, pretty woman wearing the *hijab*, the Muslim headscarf.

 ### Samir

Preparing

I came to England a couple of years ago. I had never been here before. Soon after I got here I married my wife. Her family are originally from my country but she became a British citizen a long time ago.

At first I spent so many months doing nothing except preparing documents to get the permission to stay here. There were lots and lots of documents that I took to the authorities. Everything about me - all my papers, like birth certificate, driver's licence, identity papers, my qualifications and so on. It took several months to get them all processed, going back and forth about them to the authorities. Then at last it was all done. That felt really good, because at last I was in England with all my papers organised. It was a huge effort to do it all but it made me feel there wouldn't be any problems after that.

So I have an official document proving that I have the legal right to live and even to work in England now. That's very important to me. I take it everywhere with me, because you never know when you will need it. For instance if the police stopped me or anything I would show them that immediately. It's very important to help me find a job, too.

Back home in Africa I was an IT engineer, working on IT hardware systems. I've always been crazy about repairing any equipment like that. If you have any machine at home that doesn't work, just bring it to me! Since I was a youngster, I've always loved taking them apart and figuring out how they work and putting them back together, fixed. And I always especially loved anything to do with computers. We had computers quite early on in our capital city and around the university there.

So ever since I arrived in England, I've been applying for jobs and doing job interviews. But it's been very hard to get a job, and I haven't got one yet. I have been applying not just for jobs I'm qualified for like IT, but also just for anything - like stocking shelves at Tesco and so on. But it's very hard to get those jobs even, because so many people still want them even though they're not very good jobs and the pay is very low.

Several times they have said to me 'Your application is good and you seem good but sorry, we won't be taking you because you've never worked before in this country.' That's why it's so hard - they'll always take someone who has already worked in this country.

At the start as well there was also a terrible problem with my National Insurance number. The employers would say to me 'You seem good but we won't take you unless you have a National Insurance number'. Legally I did have the right to have a National Insurance number but I just couldn't get anyone to give it to me. It was terrible and it went on for *months*.

I'd go to the Job Centre over and over and ask them for a National Insurance number. But they would say 'No, you will get that from the employer when an employer gives you a job.' But the employers would say 'No, you must have a National Insurance number before we would give you a job.' It was very upsetting for us and it went on for months.

In the end an officer at the Job Centre could see what was happening and he did the application for me, applying to the national office where they produce these National Insurance numbers. It wasn't really his job to do it but he kindly did it for me because he could see it was holding everything up. My wife and I were also going in all the time as well to the Council's housing office applying for housing. And that was being held up as well by this National Insurance number.

But I was so, so happy the day it arrived. I couldn't believe I had it at last. It made me feel more part of the system, and that now things could move and could work better for getting a job and getting housing.

It's been so hard finding a place to live since we got married. We have made many, many visits to the Council's housing office. The officers there know us very well now, and we know them very well! We did all the things you have to do to apply for housing. There are a lot of documents that you have to give - all your papers. It took months of going in and out to the office because it was all stopped waiting for my National Insurance number. But in the end they said that we wouldn't get any housing because there were too many other people waiting.

There is a very long list of people waiting to rent those flats and houses. We thought that because we have so little money and I'm unemployed and I can't receive any state benefits - that because of all that they might be able to give us something to rent, but no.

They told us we had to get a flat in the private market so we started looking there. We looked at lots and lots of places but they were all too expensive for us. In the end we had to take the flat we're living in now. It's very small - a little one-bedroom flat. But it's very nice. It's in one of these new housing developments in the city. It was the cheapest we could find, but it's still £850 a month just for the rent.

Living on little

So my wife and I have very little money to live on. We have to just live on her salary which is very small. I can't receive any unemployment benefit or housing benefit or anything like that. I don't receive any state benefits of any sort. Her salary after tax is about £1300 a month. Out of that our rent is £850. That leaves us £450 for both of us to live on and pay all household bills, food, transport, etc. It's not much.

But we're very happy. I'm so, so happy to be living here with my wife. I'm so happy to know that I'll be living here in England for the rest of my life. And I know things will get easier all the time - when I get a job, and my English improves, and I can study to improve my qualifications and get a better job, and so on. And now my wife is getting some housing benefit to top up her salary and help pay part of the rent. So that helps a lot too. My wife works full-time, but she has really struggled to find a job with better pay. But we just get on with our lives and don't take too much notice of it.

My main languages are Arabic and French but I've been working very hard at learning English. I had studied English for years already when I

came here last year. But English at school is very different from the way people speak it here! Here they talk *very*, very fast and I get very confused. But every month now my English gets much better. Now I can understand almost everything people are saying to me. With my wife we try to speak

English together mainly, to make progress. But it's funny - I could always understand *her* English so easily, even when I couldn't understand other people.

I bought a lot of CDs and books to study English with. So I try to study them at home every day for a few hours. I tried to find English classes I could go to but they're very, very expensive. At one Cambridge community college they were about £1,000 just for one term! It's too much for me. I also went to the Job Centre and asked them if they had any English classes where I could improve my English, but they don't. That really surprised me. I thought they would want people who are looking for jobs to speak good English.

But my English is getting much better. A few months ago I had to meet with an official and I couldn't speak to her much at all and there was a lot I couldn't understand. Then about six months later we met again and I was able to talk to her all the time for more than an hour and understand everything she said! Then last week we had a group meeting for some volunteering I'm doing and I could understand everything the *group* said, even when they were all talking fast and not talking to me at all! So now I can say: 'I have no problem with English!'

My life before

I have a qualification in IT, for working with hardware repair, installation and networking. The education system in my country had a lot of links with the British education system. So a lot of our qualifications, like from school and university, are the same, which is good. Back home I was around computers already in the 1980s. It's not a new thing in our capital city, where I lived - for instance, they had computers at the university there since the 1980s. But that was all before the war of course, in peace-time when the country was in a good condition.

I was used to having a good job and a good lifestyle. My family had an extremely big house - very big compared to any houses or flats in Cambridge! And really huge gardens. We had a full-time gardener who lived in a lodge in the garden with his wife. It was his job to make sure our house had lots of fruit and vegetables for the kitchen every day. We always had our own oranges off our trees, ready for breakfast. They were lovely.

But it really worries me that there are large parts of the countryside now around our city back home that are no longer cultivated. They used to be cultivated very well by the people. But now they are all abandoned and the people are going hungry. It really makes me sad to see that.

My mother is a very good cook. She always wanted to do all the cooking herself, even though we had servants who could have done it. She is a wonderful woman. A very special person in our family, keeping all the family together. I miss her very much, I really do. I try to phone her a lot but it is so expensive. I hope we'll see each other again soon. Let me show you a picture of her - see, a very beautiful, special person, isn't she?

And this is a photo of my other relatives. They had a lovely big house too like ours, and land. Their children were all very good at school. I was very close to them all before I came to England, so I miss them a lot too.

We had a very nice, happy life there. So it's a big change for me to not have a job or money and to live in a very small, rented flat. But I wouldn't change anything. I'm the happiest man in the world because I'm living with my wife here. And I love Cambridge - it's such a great place.

My father was a state official high up in the public service in our country. So I grew up with the idea of public service all around me. For instance, for many years I was an auxiliary ambulance-man myself - you know, the volunteer drivers who have another job but get called in an emergency. I loved doing that. I have qualifications in paramedics and first aid as well. I just love the idea of helping people, getting active, doing things for people. I've always been like that. I like to get involved.

And I like Cambridge very much, I really do. Just look at it all around us here - everything is so clean and beautiful, and everything works so well. Even with all the problems I have had to get a job, get housing, get my National Insurance number and so on, I still love this place. It's still easier to get things done by government offices here than it is back in my country!

OK, I have had some problems with officials here in England, like I told you. But mostly they are very good. You take in your papers and they will tell you out straight how long the thing will take. Like they'll say 'It will be ready in a week', and then usually it will be ready. In my country that could take two months, but they will never tell you like that beforehand exactly how long it will take. They'll just take your papers and you have to hope that you'll get them back some day.

For instance, to get a British driver's licence in exchange for my licence from back home, I had to go to the Driving License Authority in London to give them my licence. I decided to go there myself in case it got lost in the post. And they were very nice. They took my licence, told me the number of days I would be waiting and sent me the new British one in that time. That's the sort of thing I like about England. I am looking forward to spending the rest of my life here working and living with my wife. This is my home now.

I heard about this project you are doing to reach people from different countries and backgrounds. I wanted to meet you and get involved. Talking to you a few times like this has been helpful to me because it has given me the confidence to start doing various volunteer work using my qualifications, as you suggested. Although I'm not getting paid, I just love it because it is the first time in this country that someone has *used* my work and my qualifications. I'm doing lots of different things like that as a volunteer now.

For instance I installed a computer system that was being loaned to one community activist in her home. I installed the system, the printer, helped connect it up to the internet, and showed her how to use it. She is from Africa too and had never used a computer before. But now a few months later she's typing reports and on the internet and sending emails all the time as a volunteer.

Now my community group are also organising a big exhibition about minority groups here, so I go to the meetings about that. It's great for me to be going out doing some work. And they were able to give me a reference as a volunteer, showing the volunteer work that I have done for them and that I did it well and I am keen to help. So I am hoping now that this will help with the problem with employers - when they say they can't give me a job because I have never done any work before in England...

 Samir said nothing in this interview about the circumstances that led to him leaving his country and getting the right to live in England. But he is one of the people in the book who experienced the most extreme drop in financial circumstances through fleeing his home country. As you saw, he came from a large, manor-house with servants and live-in

gardeners, and now finds himself unemployable in a tiny flat he can't afford.

Samir's relentless job-seeking was turning up no results, mainly because his English was very poor for the first few years. Despite his good education and his efforts to improve his English, he just didn't have that fast natural aptitude for languages evident in someone like Ruth, the first interviewee (who had never had any formal education at all). Maybe over-optimistic, Samir seemed to have assumed that his knack with machinery would transfer itself to the mechanics of English, and that he'd quickly get his English up to a professional standard. But even a few hours stacking shelves at Tesco remained impossible to attain.

Behind his cheerfulness and gratitude, we get a glimpse of what the labyrinths of bureaucracy are like for new arrivals. Few of the other interviewees describe this, but they've all experienced it - the stomach-churning sensation that your whole future life depends on a particular piece of paper that someone behind this particular counter may be about to give you, or not.

Samir was used to the infamously corrupt society and governance structure in his home country. Coming as he did from a privileged rank with friends in high places, Samir gave me the indefinable sensation that he thought courting links with me should give him a leg up in this new world of Cambridge. I never felt that from any of the other interviewees. Samir knew I had some connections with the various authorities and agencies that he was chasing for documents, housing, benefits, job-offers and so on. But when I explained to him that here in England there was nothing I or anyone else could do to bend those systems in his favour, I felt I was speaking to deaf ears.

From seeing behind the scenes of these institutions in Cambridge, I knew that at least in this city, things like social housing, benefits, work-permits, jobs in the public sector - these were allocated through rigid, objective assessments that processed thousands of applicants at a time. The processes were copper-fastened with transparent audit-trails to prevent anyone receiving any special advantage.

It seemed to me that this vast, anonymous machinery was the right way to do it, to ensure fairness in dispensing increasingly scarce public resources to those who needed them most acutely. But I got the impression that Samir was steeped in a culture where having personal connections with, and doing favours for, officials was the only hope of getting the roles, documents and outcomes that you wanted.

Chapter 5

Fatima

From a Sharia regime

You can close the city gates, but you can't close the people's mouths

Saying from Fatima's country

 Fatima made contact with me over the phone. Later, after we've gotten to know each other a bit through several phone conversations, she gives me her interview over the phone too. I will never meet her face to face. She contacted me after hearing about my work and wants to tell her story, but she is clear that she doesn't want to meet. Her voice is rapid-fire, urgent and fast. Throughout the whole long call she never pauses for breath, and she hangs up suddenly at the end.

Basically, Fatima had to flee from her country solely because she wanted to live with some of the ordinary freedoms that western women enjoy. But she lived under a Sharia regime. After many conflicts with the authorities in her country, she finally decided to renounce Islam. This *apostasy* - the act of deciding that she no longer wanted to be a Muslim - made her a target for execution in her country.

So she was given asylum to save her from a form of religious persecution, but it was one that was almost entirely focused on her gender. A man in her society would have received the same punishments for apostasy, but the reason for her apostasy was that she wanted the same day to day freedoms that were enjoyed by the Muslim men around her. Her experience is a much more extreme example of a similar flight made by the woman coming up in the next chapter, who also had to flee her country because of religious legislation banning certain freedoms that women in western societies usually take for granted.

From my phone conversations with Fatima, it seems to me that she has been left with particularly poor mental health as a result of her experiences. I don't mean that she's delusional - just permanently over-wrought, unable to relax. And her solidarity with others' suffering is actually harming her further now. She is obsessed, altruistically, with the ongoing suffering of others in the country she came from and elsewhere.

Listening to Fatima's' story, you start to see how in certain restrictive regimes (though by no means all), restrictions are targeted much more heavily against women than against men. In the regime that Fatima came from, the willingness and ability to bend without question to severe, life-long restrictions was the price of life for every woman - the only way a woman could live out her life in that environment.

But in Fatima, I got the sense of a woman who - in an innate, almost biological way that was inherent in her character - simply could not bend to irrational tyranny, even when her life literally depended on it. She just could not accept what she saw as the ridiculous delusions of those who dominated her. And even to this day here in England, whenever she saw injustice or inequality, she simply could not shut up about it.

It was like an uncontrollable mechanism in her, as if she physically could not stop her mouth speaking up, speaking out. Her mouth kept on going, demanding that the world around her return to common-sense, even in situations where for a woman's mouth to go on speaking like that is to march open-eyed into catastrophe, as she had done.

Fatima

The dangers of speaking freely

When I heard about your work - that you were looking for people from other cultures to tell you about their experiences - I knew immediately I had to contact you. I just grabbed the phone straight away to talk to you like this. I always wanted something like this - someone like you in a position of higher authority to *just listen* patiently. This feels like a wonderful opportunity for me. It's really wonderful what you're doing because what I find above all here in England is that people just *don't want to listen*, but you do.

They're very polite and all that and they'll leave you alone. But the one thing they don't want to do here is *really listen* about how things are in other parts of the world - places other people come from. They just want to get on with their own life, and they want you to get on with yours, and they just don't want to think at all about the terrible things going on in some other parts of the world - really terrible things.

And it's not just back in my country that terrible things are happening. All over the world there are places where people are tortured and locked up, killed even, just for practising their religion or opposing the government, or even just for being a woman trying to live a normal woman's life!

Really, you can't imagine the sufferings of women in my country under Sharia law. It's really awful. And the west just turns a blind eye to it and lets them get on with it. When I myself managed to escape from my country and eventually got asylum here in Cambridge, I started to try to make people aware of what is going on in my country against women. But it's very difficult to get people to take any notice. Western governments just accept what's going on, so what can you do?

If I talk to you, you will have to change my name and not reveal the specific country I come from. I need total anonymity. I feel very frightened even talking to you now but I feel I must speak out, now that I have the opportunity. You can imagine all the reasons I'm frightened.

I have family still back in my own country. And of course the authorities in my country won't tolerate any criticism, especially from a woman. But then remember the Muslim community here in England won't tolerate these criticisms of Muslim states either! And then on top of that the English government are the same, and won't tolerate public criticism of Muslim states. Here in Cambridge I will tell you how even the local authorities - the Council and so on - just won't allow any public voice on the injustices I'm talking about, so as not to 'offend' Muslims in England!

So I am in danger on every single side for speaking out like this. You can just begin to imagine the hatred of fundamentalist Muslims for a woman like me, a former Muslim, who has renounced Islam. It is unthinkable to them, and puts me and those associated with me in real danger.

That is why you cannot publish who I am or exactly where I come from. But all across the Muslim states of the Middle East, North Africa and even here in Britain you will find women like me suffering, though they are silent.

These are very complex issues. I'm very glad you're doing this project. But after thinking about it a lot I've decided I would need to be completely anonymous in speaking to you. There are many reasons. I am very passionate about wanting certain truths to be heard and acknowledged by the public here in Britain and in the west. I am really devoted to that. For that I would have to show you the ways that these truths are silenced and refused and avoided even here in Cambridge - right here and now, in this city, by the authorities and the public. I can show you the facts about that. If I am to tell the truth, and to myself have good morality, then I must say these things you may not want to hear.

But at the same time it's complex because there are also so many things I really appreciate about this country - things I am so grateful for. I am *so* much better off here and so much happier than I could ever be back in my own country. I honestly believe English people are very compassionate and caring. And I am so grateful that this country has given me refuge here, and made a safe place for me with food and housing. But much more than that, the freedoms here in this society mean I've been able to explore and search and develop so much more as an individual since I came here. I've been able to search into myself and into the meaning of life and find my own way about how I want to develop as a human being, and what morality and religion I choose to follow.

Never in a million years would that have been possible back in my own country. I'd be stoned to death for putting such questions and doing such exploring!

So I'm very grateful for all that, but I also need to point out some facts about the way certain truths are suppressed by the authorities here. If I care about this society here in Britain and want to really be a part of it and contribute to it, then I have to contribute my criticisms too when I think something is going wrong, and make these views heard.

And there are others around me too who get upset at me speaking out. For instance my family, most of whom are now in another western country. I told them on the phone about your project and that I'd been speaking to you, and they were very upset that I was speaking.

Also, I want to make clear that I don't want anything for me personally out of this. It's not a goal for me that my name, my face, my personal story be put in the limelight and made a fuss of. It's important to me not to seek any personal benefits from things and to just to get on quietly with spiritual training to develop non-violence and compassion in myself.

Cambridge as an international place

All my friends now are international people from around the world. At this stage in my life, I no longer care really whether you're from my country or you're British or Malaysian or Chinese or Irish or whatever. I'm only interested in universal morality and compassion now, and trying to stop torture and persecution wherever it's happening in the world.

For instance, I practice meditation, and my main spiritual teacher is Chinese. My mother came from Yemen, and now lives in another country in the west. My best friends are English. And my fellow-meditators here in Cambridge are lots of different nationalities: Chinese, Malaysian, American, Russian and so on. One of my friends here is a wonderful older Russian woman - someone full of life and life-experiences. I feel a lot in common with her because she fled from the Soviet regime and has lived in Cambridge for a long time. We all gather at her house sometimes to practice meditation.

But probably my favourite people have always been Welsh and English. I was married to a Welshman for some time here in Britain, where his family lived as well. And his mother and sister, themselves Welsh migrants here in England, were *so wonderful* to me, they really were. And their Irish neighbours across the street as well. That was not so long after I had come here from my country and they *welcomed* me so much and looked after me so tenderly - as if I were their own daughter. Although my ex-husband and I have been separated now for a long time I think I'll never forget that woman, my mother-in-law. She was one of the kindest, warmest human beings I've ever met.

There are many refugees and other immigrants from my country here in Southern England and in Cambridge. But you must realise that there are huge differences and divergences of opinion between us. You can't for a moment just put us all together and assume we'll have the same attitudes, values or beliefs. Identities within my country are very diverse: even within the country, not to mind among those of us abroad. As well as Islam, we have populations with Turkish, Arabic, Farsi, Jewish and Christian traditions, who are all are completely different from each other. So whenever I meet someone from my country abroad, I have to approach them very carefully to get a sense of which 'sides' they are on.

Are they devout Muslims? If so they won't like me, who has renounced the Muslim faith. Muslim women almost never do this. The implications are huge of course for how I'm viewed by Muslim fundamentalists. Remember it's very, very rare for a Muslim woman to openly and actively renounce the Muslim faith as I have done. Under Sharia law, the penalty for that can be death!

And if they are Muslims, are they moderates or do they believe fully in applying Sharia law? If they proudly say they are Muslims and criticise me for leaving the Muslim faith, I have to ask them 'Do you really know what you believe in? Do you realise the full implications of applying Sharia law - how violent and cruel it is?' Those discussions with my compatriots here in Britain are not easy, I can tell you!

And then there are people from my country here in England who are wealthy and just enjoy all the secular freedoms they have here in Britain that they wouldn't have back home, and they just don't want to stir up any trouble. They're OK, so they forget about everyone else - how millions of others, especially women, are still suffering terrible abuses.

I'm different from that. I cannot just think of myself and just get on with enjoying my own life. I feel deeply connected to these other people who are still suffering under repressive regimes. Just because I managed to escape isn't the end of the story for them - it's going on still every single day for them. And that's why I want so much for the British government and the authorities to let us speak out openly about these things, rather than just collaborating with these cruel regimes and their propaganda.

For instance one day in Cambridge I saw two women from my country standing in the street. They were handing out information about our country and trying to communicate with the public. They had come up from London to do this. I went to talk to them and look at the flyers and photos they were handing out. For instance I thought it might be about the persecution of women in our country. I asked them if they were Muslims, and why. And they explained they were, and that they believe in the peaceful preservation of life. But as I looked more closely at their information I saw that they were supporters of the jihadists!

I said: 'And the jihadists - are they not taking human lives?!' I caught a glimpse too of one photo and tried to look at it but they pulled it away to hide it. I said `Why are you putting that photo away?', and I saw it. It was of a woman being stoned. And of course the jihadists are all in favour of Sharia law, which has women stoned to death for things that would be considered perfectly normal behaviour for a woman in Britain. And these two women weren't critical of that. They were trying to drum up support for them! That gives you an idea of the differences of opinion between us compatriots abroad!

I tried to talk to them about how all human rights abuses are important, everywhere, internationally, and I tried to talk about China as an example. But when I mentioned China, they just switched off and weren't interested at all and told me to go away. They were only interested in their own little corner. I find that very frustrating, very narrow-minded. Then it's only to do with politics.

Persecuted faiths

Nowadays I practice a form of Buddhism that was developed in China. It advocates non-violence, universal compassion and tolerance. A big part of our training is meditation, and our task is to practice non-violence and universal compassion all over the world, no matter what circumstances we find ourselves in. Our teachers absolutely forbid us to be involved in politics in any way. Our path is only about practicing compassion, loving-kindness and basic universal morality, no matter what our nationality or what country we're in or what is happening with political regimes.

However, the communist authorities in China see Buddhist practitioners as a threat to the communist regime. Because loving-kindness, meditation and non-violence can make people very strong and serene, which attracts others to the practice. So the communist regime has committed some really terrible human rights abuses against practitioners, just like they did against the Buddhist monks and nuns of Tibet.

The Chinese government have been quite successful at this, because of course they are very powerful and exert huge influence on other governments all over the world, including western democratic governments. So their propaganda has infiltrated western countries quite well.

But as well as simply doing our practice, I myself want to show proof of the human rights abuses and horrific persecutions that meditators continue to suffer right now today in China and Tibet. We are desperate to get this information out to the public: for instance, some of my colleagues have paid £1,000 to hire private exhibition spaces, spending all their savings on it. But anywhere up and down this country, if you go to a public space or library they will all refuse to take any flyers or information about the torture of meditators in China. It's like a blanket policy.

It's the same all over the country. For instance we went to Manchester and exactly the same thing happened. And I wrote 200 letters to universities asking them for some support or some funding to publicise about the persecutions in China - and not one of them would help us.

There are some terrible cases even among my friends here in Cambridge. One of us, a Chinese woman, was standing in the street in China with her husband peacefully distributing some leaflets about meditation and the benefits of non-violence and loving-kindness meditation. They were arrested and her husband has been detained permanently in prison by the Chinese ever since. They had a small baby and she managed to escape to the west with the baby. But she has had no news of her husband now for many months, and she cannot go back to China because she would be arrested immediately on arrival.

It's ironic because of course I fled from my country because of the terrible censorship and the abuses of the fundamentalists and Sharia law. That is all behind me now. And yet now it is here in this country - in Britain, the country I respected and admired so much - that I am again being silenced and not allowed to show the truth. Britain looks very open and democratic but in the way I've described above it's actually very tightly controlled and one is prevented from speaking out, from rocking the boat. Even though this subject is so important, and so many good people are being tortured over it every day.

You know the authorities here in Cambridge publish a poster around town that's supposed to proudly represent the ethnic and cultural and religious diversity around the city. I'm sure you know it - have you seen it? It's a big poster with photos of lots of different faces. And there's a 'Muslim woman' on there, so they're making out they've represented and included 'Muslim women'. Well I can tell you that that single photo is not representative at all! So long as we are prevented from speaking out to the Cambridge public about the abuse of women under Sharia law, so long as the British government don't challenge Islamic governments about their stoning and torture and repression of women, and they keep just placating those governments instead - how can they say they're hearing and representing the Muslim women in Cambridge?

They also have Chinese faces on their poster. And they attend celebrations of Chinese culture held by the Chinese community in Cambridge. But at those celebrations the truth about the human rights abuses of the Chinese government is suppressed, isn't it? You're not allowed to show it or talk about it. You can only smile and nod and talk about how great Chinese culture is and how happy the Chinese people are. I like celebrations and positivity as much as the next person. But censorship is another matter. How can the English authorities claim they're being representative of Chinese residents here if they won't let them show the truth about the Chinese government's actions?

I think the reason the Chinese government find meditation so threatening is because it says politics and governments are irrelevant - that the only real problem in the world is a moral one, the lack of compassion and kindness and morality. That's a powerful universal message. Think what Ghandi achieved with a message like that! So it threatens a Chinese government that relies so heavily on political censorship and repression.

But I still believe that the British as individuals are compassionate people, and would be horrified by these facts. Here it's not at all like in my old country where under Sharia law, torture and censorship and repression of basic human rights are not only tolerated but are actually part of the official state law! Britain and the British people don't have that cruelty and wrong morality.

On the other hand, our exhibition was shown in the United States, where city councils hosted it, and it was very well received. People say that when they see our meditators' art-works, they feel a sense of peace and serenity and compassion emanating from them. Our exhibition really wants to show that. That despite torture and repressive regimes and so on, there are people getting together all over the world in an enlightened way, focusing on non-violence and loving kindness and doing positive things together.

Can you help us find a place to show this exhibition here? Like in a theatre or public hall? And after your book project, what I'd love to see as well is an informal exhibition where residents from different countries, cultures and faiths can show their own cultures, and everyone can mix and mingle in an informal way. I think that's much better than formal speeches on a stage and so on. I think it's a really nice atmosphere when you can have displays and people can wander about, perhaps have a drink and meet different people, exchanging points of view. That is my wish for your project!

Among my interviewees, Fatima was by far the most active here in England in terms of campaigning - agitating, even - for justice for those still suffering under the regime she had left behind. Unlike the others, who seemed more resigned, she had a mordant demand and expectation that the authorities here in England should do more to help those people. She tirelessly lobbied public agencies and prominent organisations to let her show exhibitions in their venues critiquing the regimes of those governments. She was always refused.

In her efforts to build new links outside the culture of origin that she found so punitive, after settling here she married into a migrant family of a very different ethnicity and built with the women of that family the solidarity that she had been missing. She also joined a new religion - a liberal, international one loosely based on Buddhism. But these links again brought her ongoing suffering through the intense solidarity she felt for her fellow-religionists being persecuted in China.

Even now that she herself had been safely removed from her tormentors through asylum in England, the same unstoppable mechanism was at work in Fatima's mouth when she thought of the ongoing sufferings of others back home and in other countries. She simply could not *shut it*, even though she strongly felt that that was what English society expected her to do now that she was safe herself.

Fatima reminded me of a whole blend of mythical, archetypal female figures who *could not stop*. Like Scheherazade, the Arabian woman who told stories all night long, night after night, to distract her would-be executioner. Or Cassandra, the Ancient Greek prophetess who couldn't stop herself seeing into future disasters as yet invisible to others. Or *The girl with the red shoes* in the Hans Christian Anderson fairy-tale: an involuntary dancer, she could not stop dancing while she wore the red shoes, and she couldn't get them off either.

Though it doesn't come across so much in the written transcript here, Fatima was by far the most distressed and agitated of all the people I interviewed. A few other speakers had developed mental health problems from the chronic stress of their experiences, but they had been or were being successfully treated in England. I never heard whether Fatima was offered or accepted treatment for what seemed to me her rather manic mental state.

Women
your body
belongs
to you!

Chapter 6

Saoirse

From the Catholic Republic of Ireland

I have never seen a situation so dismal that a policeman couldn't make it worse

Irish playwright Brendan Behan

 *Saoirse* is not her real name. In the Irish language, it means *Freedom*. As you read her story you'll see why she chose this pseudonym. She got in touch because she'd seen a publication I had done in the past about Irish women in Britain. [15] Saoirse is successful in a demanding profession here in Cambridge, and remains active in networks campaigning on the issue that drove her out of Ireland.

At her suggestion, we meet at the University Arms, a venerable, plush, old hotel with dark wood-panelling, a grand piano, chandeliers and tall leaded windows. They look out over the *'Reality-Checkpoint'* lamp-post I was shown the week I arrived in Cambridge twenty years ago. A waiter in a waistcoat and bow-tie serves us elaborately with a silver tray of tea and hand-made biscuits. It is appropriately expensive.

Sunlight streams down on us through the high windows and dances off the silver milk-jug. Two professional Irishwomen meeting for afternoon tea in a fine hotel - what could be more natural? I curl up in the old leather armchair and ask what brought her here to England.

---

[15] Hoffman-Buckley, M., 1997. 'Sitting on your politics - The Irish among the British and the Women among the Irish'. In: *Location and Dislocation in Contemporary Irish Society - Emigration and Irish Identities*, McLaughlin, J. (ed.). Cork: Cork University Press

Saoirse

When I think back on the whole situation that meant I had to leave Ireland, I think of a quote from our compatriot Oscar Wilde: 'Friends stab you in the front'. In certain situations, those you love and who are meant to care for you can turn against you dramatically, and that was my experience of Ireland as a state.

As a young woman I *had* to come to England, for a reason I would never have expected. Growing up in Ireland, I had always learned to despise the 'Brits'. You need to understand that to know what coming here meant for me.

At school we learned about their centuries of brutality as invaders and colonisers in Ireland, using Ireland as the testing-ground for their later invasions of India, Africa and other regions. For instance the name Cromwell to Irish people where I grew up was the same as the name Hitler is to Jews. It was that simple. So I was stunned - really stunned - when I came to England and discovered that here he is not seen as an evil, shameful figure. I still am stunned about that, really.

My grandparents on both sides had fought in Ireland's War of Independence, so growing up you heard all the horror-stories from the horse's mouth, as it were. You heard what it was like around 1920 in our area. The English still held our whole country occupied by military force. Then they unleashed what were called the 'Black & Tans' on the local people - that was when they emptied English prisons, sending the prisoners to fight the local Irish villagers who were rebelling. We had had the 'Black & Tans' in our area, and the name alone struck fear into your heart as a child, when I was growing up.

Then all through the 1970s and 80s when I was a young person, every night on the TV news in Ireland, the first three minutes or so were just a routine roll-call of all the people who had been blown up, 'kneecapped', kidnapped or executed in the war in Northern Ireland that day. I guess in that conflict, whether rightly or wrongly, we saw the British Army as the modern equivalent of the 'Black & Tans'. And recent public inquiries by the British government into events of that time like Bloody Sunday do tend to confirm that - even they admit that the British Army often acted illegally, murdering innocent Irish civilians.

This was also the era when the young Irish political prisoners like Bobby Sands were left to die by Margaret Thatcher in the internment jails in Northern Ireland. They weren't asking for release - only that it be admitted that they were *political* prisoners, not common criminals. That was a long protracted agony, to see their deaths by starvation unfolding on television.

Here in England it was the era when Irish people were being interned without trial, with whole families and groups of acquaintances locked away for decades for crimes they were later proven innocent of, and released. You wrote about that in the earlier publication of yours that I read. [16] The *Birmingham Six*, the *Guildford Four* and so on - innocent people whose lives were ruined just for being Irish in England at that time.

So no, there was nothing positive about my view of England as a young person - really nothing at all, I'm sorry. I know now that this is all so very far from how English people see themselves. I was amazed too when I met people here from around the world and found out that in many parts of the world, England was or is seen as a model of 'fair play', democracy and justice. Nothing could be farther from our historical experience of them in Ireland. We saw them as a dangerous, barbaric nation to be avoided.

But I think too that Irish culture raises people to have a much, much stronger and longer sense of history than English culture does. In Ireland, centuries - even millennia - of history are just part of people's everyday world-view. It's just a natural part of the air you breathe. So with that vivid sense of memory, you judge nations on a much longer perspective than just the present moment. Whereas English people seem to me to be raised and educated in a much more amnesiac way, with very little information about

---

[16] Cited in footnote 15 on page 110.

the violence and traumas their invasions inflicted on other countries over the past 150 years, which would be considered *recent* time in Ireland. The English wouldn't even know what I mean when I say their 'invasions', because their word for that is the 'British Empire', something they're actually proud of…

Leaving Ireland

As a young woman I'd enjoyed visiting countries on the continent but I used to avoid England as a dangerous place - an uncivilised nation that I planned never to have to pass through. It's ironic, obviously, that I've ended up spending most of my life here.

Anyway, that's where I was at as a single young person when I had the misfortune to suddenly find myself accidentally pregnant in the Ireland of the 1980s. It was horrific. It's very hard to describe or convey now how impossible it felt at that time to contemplate having a child as a young single woman in Ireland. I went on to have much-wanted children later in life but at that point there was not a single fibre of my being that wanted that pregnancy. I would have done anything - whatever it took - to get out of that pregnancy in that society as a single woman at that time.

It was impossible of course to tell your family or anyone in the locality as they would have kicked you out straight away. I remember standing in a hallway at the GP surgery in Ireland where I got the test-result, and the faces standing around me - doctors and nurses and so-called 'counsellors' - and me pleading 'Isn't there *anyone* who can help me?' and all the faces turning away and shutting their doors.

This was a time when anyone who gave you the phone number of an abortion hospital in England, for instance, would go to prison for it in Ireland. The Irish government used to cut out the back pages of women's magazines at Dublin airport before letting them into the country for sale in Ireland, so that no-one could get the phone numbers. Isn't that pathetic? And of course there was nothing like the internet then for ordinary people. No-one could get information if the government didn't want you to have it.

The very odd thing is that though I remember all this so vividly, I cannot remember who it was that helped me a few weeks later - that saved me by getting the phone number of a Marie Stopes Clinic in England into my hand somehow. Maybe I've blotted out just that bit to protect those kind people somehow, whoever they were, who took that risk for me. And of course many brave people did go to jail on purpose later for that - for passing the phone number of an English abortion hospital to women in Dublin who needed it, while knowing they'd go to jail for it. They wanted to make that point.

Some years later things got much worse in Ireland, rather than better, when they made it a crime to even be caught trying to leave Ireland if the Irish authorities even *suspected* that you *might* be planning to have an abortion abroad. It was insane, in the modern era when Ireland otherwise such a sophisticated, educated, international country. There was just no excuse for it. And Lord protect us, there was then that case of little 'X', the raped child who was intercepted at Dublin airport by the police while travelling with her parents to get a termination in England. Some medical bastard tipped the police off, apparently. And they captured her and made her a prisoner of the state so that she couldn't escape abroad to get out of that pregnancy, and she would have to go through with it.

Bloody neanderthals. Shame and disgrace on them. It brings tears of rage and shame to my eyes to think of it - shame on them before all the nations of the world - there is no possible excuse for it, in a modern, highly-educated, well-off country in the western world. So you see now how things can flip over, depending on which issue you're addressing? Who's the barbaric nation now?!

So anyway I made that blessed phone call, got my appointment, borrowed the money and made my way to England in secret without anyone knowing. I arrived in England and was met by the kindest people you can imagine. It was unbelievable. A network - of volunteers, I suppose - had this whole system in place just to look after women like me coming over from Ireland for this purpose. They took me to a special B&B near the hospital that was like a 'safe haven' for women 'on the run' like this from

Ireland. And the owner was just so polite and cheerful and respectful and treated me like a normal person even though she knew everything that was going on and it was then - just from the normal, kind way she was with me, that I knew everything was going to be ok. I had no fear whatsoever. I could just feel that these people were truly civilised, adult people. Christ, to say it was a breath of fresh air would be a big understatement. I just felt that everything about the way they approached the subject was - well, just *grown-up*. Not making a huge big deal of it, not making my personal situation into some kind of insane national drama of religion and politics…

At the clinic next day you had to have a long interview - up to a couple of hours, I remember - with their psychologist, to ensure that you were right for the operation. That you weren't having the abortion against your will, you wouldn't regret it, you were well enough and so on. She was a relaxed, intelligent person: professional but human at the same time, not hiding behind some sort of institutional 'mask' or role.

We had a long chat in which I convinced her heartily that no, I would not regret this termination. We even laughed a bit at the end when she conceded that yes, there was definitely no ambiguity about how I felt about it. And I thought 'That's right - that's how it should be - it should be a free choice, not an inescapable nightmare'.

After the operation, I had an odd experience as I was waking up in the recovery room. I didn't know where I was or why I was there. Someone was standing right beside me - I could feel their warmth steady against my arm. The room was filled with sunlight and I felt like I was floating pleasantly. The voice beside me - a woman's voice - said quietly, almost in my ear: 'I know why you're so happy'. And I thought 'Oh yes, that's what this sensation is called in words - *happy*.' And I realised 'God, yes, I do feel *soooo* happy.' During the previous weeks of torment, I'd forgotten you could feel that way. It was such a strong physical sensation - I could have screeched with happiness.

But then I thought about her words: what did they mean? '*I know why you're so happy*.' And only then it hit me. Oh yes, oh God, it's *happened*, it's done, it's all over – the thing I have dreamed of has happened in reality!

These people have rescued me. They have delivered me back to myself. That longed-for operation is done and they have delivered me back to myself - just me and myself in my own body. Christ almighty, that's why I'm so happy! I have received what I needed. These kind strangers intervened and gave it to me. The joy and relief and gratitude were indescribable.

And I thought it was odd - though sweet - that that nurse's words could see right through me into my soul and name what I was feeling even before my own brain had processed it fully. Presumably I had a huge smile on my face even before fully waking up, and that was what she was reacting to. It was as if the 'good news' was there in my body before consciously reaching my brain. Because of course it was my body that had had the problem and needed liberating, not my brain. And they had returned my body to me, its rightful owner.

I was aware afterwards that the nurse's remark could seem unprofessional or inappropriate but it was just a spontaneous human connection that that person standing there happened to make with the very depths of my heart. It was like being 'greeted with a smile' or welcomed with open arms as I arrived back into the land of the living, from the semi-death that I had experienced in that so-unwanted pregnancy. I felt reborn, as if their operation had delivered me back into my own life.

Paradoxes

So you see... My views on English society and Irish society were flipped on their head by those experiences. I don't know what more to say to show you how much it all meant to me - I hope I've conveyed it. How betrayed and let down I felt by Irish society. So who was the enemy now?! That was a real paradox for me, one that I still haven't reconciled to this day really.

England had given me refuge and rescued me in my darkest hour, as of course it has done quietly for hundreds of thousands of Irish women who have come here for terminations over so many decades. A book has been written about it, called *Ireland's Hidden Diaspora*. [17] I suppose most of those women creep back into Ireland and get on with their lives, but I couldn't. I was revolted by the place after that, and especially later with the 'X case' and the legislation that was made even more draconian.

I did go back straight after the operation so as not to raise any suspicions around me in Ireland. But I left immediately afterwards, came over here to get work and ended up staying to this day.

Does that sound very strange? I just feel I could not live in Ireland so long as that legislation remains in place there. It's too brutal. It's too hypocritical of them, considering they know full well that their terminations are just 'exported' to England, who looks after all those women for them.

They deliberately let a young Indian doctor die there in hospital a couple of years ago, didn't they, rather than end the pregnancy that was killing her as she lay there in the hospital bed. She thought she was passing through Ireland for a few years, just to work there. To me they are savages, people who will do that today, while having all the modern facilities and prosperity to prevent it.

I know that sounds extreme. Am I a very extremist person to have those views? I don't know. I admire all the people in Ireland who carry on campaigning for women's *right to choose*. They are badly needed. But I couldn't live there like they do. For me, Ireland will only be a civilised country once a woman's right to choose is law there. I'd be quite happy to move back and retire there then - I enjoy the *'ceol, caint agus craic'* as much as the next person! [18]

So *that* was Saoirse's story... I hadn't guessed what it was going to be about. We finish our tea in companionable,

[17] Rossiter, A., 2009. *Ireland's Hidden Diaspora - The Abortion Trail and the Making of a London-Irish Underground, 1980-2000.* New York: IASC Publishing

[18] An Irish-language expression meaning the music, conversation and social banter that are at the heart of Irish culture

thoughtful silence. There's a sense of peace and calm again, like after a storm, as if she had really needed to air all those fiercely-felt memories, as well as the strong feeling that she retains to this day about the law in Ireland.

I think most educated, professional women in western Europe would agree with her views. I say this to her. That I don't think she needs to feel she's particularly 'extreme'. We shrug about it with a sad smile.

As I walk away from her outside the hotel, it occurs to me that maybe the biggest theme in this book is the ambivalence *anyone* can feel towards any given country, whether their country of origin or their host country as an immigrant. Nation states are complex things, with favourable and unfavourable aspects. And even if a state regime is brutal, the *culture* that the state is imposed upon and overlaying may well be a wonderful one. Most of my interviewees had loved most aspects of their home countries. They tended to love the culture, the landscape, the language, the food, the people, the music, even the religion - it was just the tyranny and persecution that they didn't like.

I don't know whether Saoirse 'loved' Ireland. As an Irish person myself, I have loved Ireland as a culture and felt proud of it in many ways. Like Saoirse, I saw its wars as resistance movements and civil rights movements against a mighty foreign invader. And the 'craic' is indeed very good there.[19] But I had hated the ridiculous leeway given to church abuses in Ireland. I hated the church's mistreatment of sexuality. And I hated the church-state's repressive legislation against reproductive rights. In a tiny country, that's a lot to hate. So I'd been quite happy to emigrate at the end of my teens and leave it behind in favour of the wider world.

---

[19] The Gaelic word 'craic' means Irish people's sense of fun and laid-back enjoyment of life.

Chapter 7

Habibah

From West Africa

Don't blame God for creating the tiger - thank him for not giving it wings
Saying from Habibah's country

 Enticing aromas drift in from the tiny, spotless kitchenette where Habibah is making me coffee. As a fan of good coffee, I'm looking forward to this one. It's from West Africa, where she comes from. She has just ground the beans and the aromatic coffee is now bubbling away over the stove in a little metal pot with a pod of cardamom.

She comes in, leaning heavily on her walking stick, carrying a plate of crescent-shaped biscuits made of almond and cinnamon, each crowned with a bright green pistachio nut, fresh out of her oven.

While she pours the coffee, I look around the Aladdin's cave of her little studio-flat. Like a temporary storage-room, it is crammed from floor to ceiling with expensive-looking, exotic furniture and ornaments. More Versailles than Africa, the sheen of these things reminds me of the apartments of very wealthy people that I've visited in Paris or Geneva. Book-cases, standing lamps, elaborate vases perch precariously on every available surface, crowding in around us where we sit on this elegantly upholstered *chaise longue*. The only things you can deduce from this incongruous environment are that Habibah was once immersed in wealth and glamour, that she has managed to transport some of the relics of it here to her tiny council flat, and that she still enjoys these displaced, piled-up little luxuries, rather than feeling saddened by them in this humbled setting.

Habibah herself has the same gleaming elegance as the objects around her. Despite age, physical pain, loss of mobility and whatever other losses brought her here, she sits upright, immaculately dressed in expensive-looking clothes, a sort of Parisian *bourgeoise* crossed with jet-setting Africa. Her black skin, hair and eyes and her red-polished nails still glow with vitality. She still has the energy, intelligence and verve of an international *lady*.

Both the biscuits and the coffee taste extraordinary, the best I've ever had in Cambridge. She was right when she said that a single cardamom pod would make the rich, strong coffee somehow smoother, kissed with a gentle sweetness. The crumbly, fragrant biscuits melt on the tongue with no aftertaste of sugar or fat. Settling back on the *chaise longue* with nothing to do for the afternoon but listen and receive her story, I ask Habibah about her life before she came here.

Habibah

Exchange between cultures in Africa

Oh, my family in Africa believed in girls getting a good education. Education was very important to them. My mother was a doctor at the capital's hospital. Our extended family were all well qualified too and held very good jobs - consultant doctors, judges, accountants, politicians... They mostly got their training and qualifications in Europe, in European languages. We had many different institutes back home that taught European languages - institutes to learn Russian, German, the *Alliance Francaise* and so on....

I was raised with a very international attitude. Around us in the capital there were Italians, Germans, French, Americans... You see our people are very hospitable by nature. They're confident in their own culture and they like to welcome and mix with others. There were none of those terrible divisions we have now based on what nationality or religion you were or what colour you were or what language you spoke.

I was sent to an international school because my parents wanted me to get a good education and that was the best school available for me. It served a lot of expatriates. A lot of American children used to go there, coming from the American army bases around Africa. On breaks and holidays, my family used to spoil us very badly, I must say! My father was a wonderful musician who taught me to play the piano. He gave me a love of music. I was able to continue studying piano right through school, and I sang in choirs as well. It was a real art that my father had learned from Italians in our country.

The thing is, I feel that there was a genuine intellectual exchange between our people and colonial cultures. They never oppressed or disrespected us, and we were able to benefit from their knowledge and education too, like in medicine and so on. The nature and tradition of our people is to be very welcoming and open and hospitable - to mingle. When you arrived among them you would straight away be invited to people's homes to come and visit and settle in. There was no idea at all of segregation - around religion or skin-colour or all that. To be honest the first we ever saw of that was when the Catholic missions started telling people 'You must do such and such. You must not celebrate such and such festivals. You must not mix with such and such people.' That was the first we had heard of that sort of attitude - of all these barriers and segregations of different sorts.

Our capital at that time was a genuine meeting point for so many different cultures and religions, embracing each other and celebrating each other's strong points. We were very lucky to live in that time - before the fundamentalists came in and destroyed everything. All that tradition of openness and tolerance and curiosity about other ways of life and religions - it's truly horrible how it was all destroyed by the fundamentalists. My grandmother used to say that by comparison 'It makes me wish those British colonials were still here instead.'

Originally as a family we were of course Muslims. But I was in so many clubs and hobbies and activities that just through my activities I was more like a Christian, culturally and socially. We had so many Jewish friends as well. We used to participate in everything! Jewish festivals, Christmas for the Christians, Ramadan for the Muslims - we used to celebrate them all in together! It seems amazing now to think of it compared to the divisions there are now in some places.

That was the beauty of our country at that time: there were none of these barriers at all. There was always some festival or other to celebrate from some religion - and everyone celebrated them all mixed in together! You'd have lunches and dinners and meals and parties to celebrate them and everyone was invited. Often you'd even stay overnight for these festivals.

We gained our independence well ahead of many other African countries that had to fight long for independence through the 60s and 70s. And we were very lucky in our city. Even when colonised, we were never oppressed in the way some other colonies were. We have positive memories of the colonial era, and there are clubs of former colonials in Europe that still maintain excellent relations with our country and send money to support projects there.

War-zones

It was only when I moved around to live and work in many different African countries that I saw oppression for the first time. It was amazing how different things were in different countries. For instance in the Congo, the people were of a very relaxed nature - very calm and collected. You could think you were living in an African version of France. The food, the language, the attitudes of the Congoans were all very French and there was a very easy-going atmosphere. Nigeria I would say was the opposite. There was a high level of criminality and a sense that the society was quite dangerous. People were a lot less trusting, relaxed and open. That led to a lot of black magic sort of practices too.

We arrived in Harare in Zimbabwe five years after independence and there I was so so struck by how the people had been horribly oppressed by the British colonisers there. It was new to me to see people who had suffered so much under a British colonial regime. I'd never seen any sort of apartheid until I went to Zimbabwe. At that time, just five years after independence, they weren't even beginning yet to recover from it. It was horrible, and I found it hard to be there and see it all around.

We also lived and worked in Ethiopia. I just loved the Ethiopians - such a great people. They are so, so proud of their country - ready to die for it! That was during the time of Mangisto - a horrible ruthless man and terrible tyrant. But they had a long-term, philosophical view of it and would say 'We don't care about Mangisto. One day he'll be finished and we'll have our country back.' But in that beautiful country was also the first time I saw real, extreme poverty.

I know what it is to live in a war-zone. It is really horrific. I lived in several different war-zones. I have seen it all face to face, first hand. How the people suffered - during the liberation movements in Zimbabwe, in Namibia. The suffering of the people in Ethiopia... It is unimaginable.

And of course it's the women, the children, the elderly who suffer the most. The politicians who make the decisions about war are protected, settled somewhere safe with their lives and their families. It's the very worst thing in the world - to have your home destroyed and burned.

And it's just heart-breaking to watch the bombings in the Middle East at the moment. For instance, have you ever been there, to Lebanon? I have. It's just beautiful. Such a beautiful country. They say it is the Switzerland of the Middle East.

The other day I saw on the television there was one Lebanese man and he was the sole survivor with seventeen other members of his family killed where they had taken shelter, in what was supposed to be a safe place.

Marriage

My parents lived on a big manor estate for the extended family, where the brothers were all married in, each with their own quarters. My grandfather owned a great deal of land, with a big export business from orchards and agriculture. He had set his children set up with their own families in different wings of the big house.

One day I visited a cousin nearby. At her house there was a young lawyer visiting. Apparently he spoke to her later and asked her many questions about me. He asked and asked and asked and was insistent on meeting me. He was looking for a girl to marry, of course! My cousin said 'I really don't think Habibah would suit you. You know she's studying, and she may be intent on going on to university too.'

Well anyway I took my graduation exams and I got accepted to go to university abroad. But - and this was a big but - this young lawyer had met with my brother and asked about me, then found his way to speak to my father. Now I was very lucky because my father would never force his daughter into marriage. My father told him 'Let me speak to her first and see what she's thinking.' I told my father that I wanted to go to university. And of course my family did really believe in girls getting a full education. But my father did say to me 'He is a very nice, gentle man, and he's from a very good family...' So I finally agreed to meet him. You see in those days a young man had to speak to the parents first before he could approach a girl to meet her and get to know her: in those days you couldn't just barge in!

And of course he was indeed very good, this young man! He was a very distinguished student - a 'First Class' man. He sat the Oxford and Cambridge University examinations as well as our own exams in our capital, and he got nothing but distinctions. Our university was recognised as a British School of Law, as it was connected into the British system.

And when I met him I saw he was very, very handsome! He was extremely smart-looking. He always dressed in a suit, not only when in the law-courts. And he was very well spoken because he was from a very good, well-educated family. They were MPs, judges and leading national figures.

So you knew you weren't marrying into a wishy-washy family there! That was important to me and my family. In our culture when a girl married, she really left her own family and became part of her husband's family. So the choice of family to send her to is important for her: you can't just drop your daughter on just anybody who comes along! And for our family, education was everything.

I first met my suitor at my parents' home. He then asked my father if he could take me out for tea, and because my father was very liberal he agreed. I sat the young man down and told him exactly what I wanted. That I wanted to go to university. 'So you'll have to wait', I said to him. 'Fine', he said. 'Even better, I'll book you in so you can do the Cambridge University entrance exams.'

Building international collaborations

My husband was a lecturer at our national School of Law. He was offered posts abroad but he said 'No, I must give my expertise in my own country, because they sponsored me for my training.' But he built up really good links between our national university and universities abroad, as bridges that are still being used today to help train young African lawyers. He worked all over Africa, in so many places. His role was to set up law schools. So many lawyers, solicitors, judges were trained - and are still being trained - at those places.

The liberation movement was sweeping through Southern Africa, with many countries starting to fight for their independence. Friends of ours used to deliver supplies to them out in the bush so that they could carry on. As a judge, my husband had to try to avoid getting pulled into politics, but it was difficult. He couldn't help getting stuck in to mobilise people and get things done. What was needed most urgently? For instance, great numbers of women had been displaced in the violence. You'd have a woman with five or six small children, her husband killed in the war, and displaced from her home place. And parts of Africa can be very cold in winter!

After the independence movements, there were also the first democratic elections. But there were big problems to get the tribes-people in from the Bush to the ballot boxes. People we knew were trucking the first-time voters in from the Bush to get them to the ballot boxes so they could vote. You really saw what ordinary African people can achieve when they put their mind to it.

I've always visualised the success of a project before I go into it. I just visualise the goal clearly in my head and a positive result. I don't think about what could go wrong. And my husband was very good. He was always there to support me. I'd talk to him and say 'I want to do this and this', and then he'd help me.

But as well as this work, I used to entertain constantly as well. You know when I go to any country I like to find out all about their culture, their food, their language - get a dress made in their local style and so on.

Meanwhile, my children were studying. I always used to pump them up, saying: 'Be proud of your achievements as intelligent Black youth. Stand up high with your head up and put your thinking straight! Tell people exactly what is in your head! Don't you dare think you're less than anyone else, no matter where you are. You are here on your own merit!'

Positive action

It used to be, even up to a few years ago, that you could be so proud to be living in this nation here in England. The British were world leaders in terms of politics and democracy and foreign policy. You'd say to people around the world 'I live in England' and they'd say 'Aren't you so lucky?' And I did feel that way. I was proud of this country. I still am except for the foreign policy. Now, with Britain kow-towing to the United States with all this terrible foreign policy - are we lucky? Are we proud? Are we lucky to be living in this country now under this policy? Can we be proud? I don't think so.

It's like living in a dictatorship here now: I want to say to the politicians, listen to the people. The people don't agree with the positions you're taking. Hardly anyone agrees with it. But we can't all just up and leave England in protest because of the insecurity. We have a home and work here - where would we go now?

I also totally disagree with the terrorists' approach these days, but I do understand their anger about American and British foreign policy. That's awful - just awful. It's going to bring so many problems onto this country. So I understand the anger of young Arabs and Muslims. But they must express that anger in positive ways - not by falling completely into the negative. There are so, so many ways to get involved and make a difference. They must channel that into positive action. Organise rallies and demonstrations, get active, get involved in the political process. I know the political process can seem slow but ultimately it is the only way!

You know we supported liberation movements all across Africa, so that the people could live in democracies they elected themselves. That was the only way to do it. People personally went out there into the Bush for days on end to get people to the ballot-boxes so they could vote in their first ever democratic elections.

And those people - in Zimbabwe, Namibia, South Africa and other countries - they did have to fight to create a democratic state. There was suffering. Their independence fighters went out into the bush and fought from outside, and it was hard for the people inside. But they got there. The fighting was kept to a minimum and they never targeted anyone else, dragging anyone else into it, only those directly involved.

Whereas this international terrorist movement now is a totally different thing. This idea of targeting masses of innocent people going about their own business, people who have nothing to do with the conflict - it's just wrong. So people are so scared now, under threat all the time. One can only pray that things will settle down, and pray for people in the war zones.

And I really, really hope that this project you're doing here - listening to the lives and views of ethnic residents in Cambridge, letting them express their views as part of the dialogue in the city - I just hope this can help a little bit to open up more dialogue between the different ethnic groups and let people express themselves peacefully. I really hope we can help a little in this way.

Of course I'm alone here now, without my husband. I have serious health problems and am waiting for an operation. But I was lucky to get a social housing flat here in Cambridge. My experience was that the authorities here are very helpful - if you bring along all the exactly right papers and you speak their sort of language and so on. They offered me this tiny one-bedroom flat here. It's in a very well-kept, quiet council estate. And you see I have a lot of my own things around me - things that remind me of those many different countries and cultures I've lived in.

Local racism

However things have been so, so difficult with a few White neighbours. Once I was very poorly and couldn't look after myself so two friends slept over in my living room here to see after me. Next thing I knew I got a letter from the authorities saying there were various allegations against me and they must come to investigate! Those neighbours, without speaking to me about it, had raised a formal complaint that I was 'sub-letting' my flat!

But when the housing officer came to inspect, she couldn't believe her eyes. When she saw how I've decorated my little home in such an attractive, personal way, she could see straight away that I'd never be 'sub-letting' it to someone else! And you know, in fact I had overheard that pair of neighbours muttering between themselves about a flat being sublet, but it had never occurred to me for a moment that it was me they were talking about!

Despite my health problems I'm a very active woman. When I was left on my own I went out and found a job until I was too sick to work, and since then I've still been doing lots of volunteering in the community. I think it's sad for those neighbours if their own lives are so empty that they can only watch from behind their curtains worrying about when I come in and go out and who is calling to see me.

Literally, that woman will walk all the way around the block to avoid me. I planted some roses to brighten up the flats and when I come out to water them she'll first stare at me and then literally run away. I say hallo to her, smiling, and she'll swing her head away in the other direction not to say hallo to me.

Of course it's very unpleasant. But just try to imagine what she's thinking. I'm sure she loves her little garden and the nice area we have here, just like I do. And she thinks 'This Black woman won't know how to live in a nice place like this…She'll wreck it on us…' Maybe she thought I'd come downstairs and eat her or throw something through her letterbox, because that is how some ignorant people think about you when you're a Black woman.

When the officer came around to investigate me, she was full of apologies straight away when she saw how I live. She saw straight away that I'm a quiet, respectable person with an active life - and that these complaints came from someone with an empty, fearful life looking out from behind the curtains. The officer said to me: 'I'm really sorry about this, Habibah - it shouldn't have happened.'

All I can do now is to observe very strict rules not to give those neighbours any loophole they could complain me for. When I moved in here the housing officer said to me 'This is your home now.' And I believed them. But now I feel like I'm being spied on like a prisoner.

So we really must do something just to educate people not to be afraid of people from other cultures. Open them up a bit gently to just exchange on an ordinary human level. That's why I feel this project you're doing about ethnic residents' lives is so important and valuable. We can use it to gently navigate our way around the prejudices.

The other thing I want to do is get a couple of benches put in in the communal green space outside our block of flats. Then it could be a focal point for us neighbours to meet and socialise a little - just to sit out there together with a cup of coffee and enjoy the greenery and the birds together.

 Habibah was the interviewee who had experienced the most dramatic drop in privilege and financial circumstances. She was born into the ruling classes of her country, among the most educated, wealthy elites. Her family owned country estates, holding positions as top politicians and chief medical officers. She had been married to a judge working for international development agencies and had travelled extensively with him, mixing with heads of state in the countries they passed through.

By the time I met her, war was raging back in her country and she was living alone in a council flat in England, with serious health problems and limited mobility. But she seemed unbowed. Like some of the other interviewees, Habibah had never gotten the advanced education that she had aspired to and was expecting - life got in the way. So, like many of the others, she became an autodidact instead, teaching herself the languages, management skills and international diplomacy that enabled her to do the volunteering tasks she set herself. Also like many of the others, the extensive work that she did for the communities around her was unpaid - it was voluntary work that came from an inner urge to contribute rather than the building of a career.

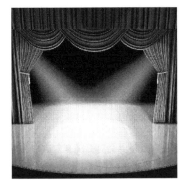

Chapter 8

Fionn

From the 'Troubles' in Northern Ireland

As you slide down the banister of life, may the splinters never point the wrong way
Irish saying

'*Céad míle fáilte romhat, a stór, conas 'tá tú? Nach bhfuil tú go hálainn ar fad inniu! Tar isteach, tá an tae réidh...*'

'*Go raibh maith agat*', I mutter in reply, taken by surprise. Fionn knows I'm Irish so I'm assuming he doesn't greet everyone who comes to the door like this - *as Gaeilge*! [20]

Though a pensioner, he's still an attractive man. He has a twinkling eye and ripples with Irish charm. As I cross the threshold, stepping into his little rented flat with my clipboard under my arm, a wave of forgotten memory suddenly washes through me. I recall how, after emigrating to France in my late teens, for years afterwards I found Irish men extraordinarily attractive, when I met them abroad or on visits to the island.

It was like a magnet, pulling on ancestral instincts in the way an MRI scanner pulls on your body's electrons. Today, for the first time, I suddenly wondered: do other emigrants feel that about their compatriots too? I thought of how many immigrants I knew here who dated and married people from their own ethnicity. I'd always assumed that was just a cultural thing - that they understood each other and had shared values. But now for the first time I wondered - is it physical too? Do they feel that magnetic pull that I used to feel around Irish men when I first lived abroad? Keeping all that firmly to myself, I step politely into his hallway.

Here I am amazed. I know he has no money, only his small state pension to live on. But the place is like an art-gallery. Every corner is white, airy, spotless, lit by posters of luminous art-works in elegant frames. With a little inner gulp, I resolve to make my home look and feel like this too. Elegant, inspiring, with a clean and sparkling energy. So much for my assumption that an elderly bachelor would live in squalor!

He seats me with tea and his homemade cake. We eat in easy silence for a while, enjoying the haven of tranquillity he has created. I switch on the microphone and ask him what he thinks of life here in England, compared to how things were - or are - 'back home'.

---

[20] As *Gaeilge* means 'in the Irish language'.

Fionn

Oh, *'Sex Kitten For Personal Use!'* - that's the first thing I remember seeing on the day I arrived in London - on a sign in a phone-box. *Sex Kitten For Personal Use!* Stuck up in a phone-box - *Imagine!* (We laugh a lot.) I've never forgotten it. That was a billion miles away from the repressed Catholic culture I was coming from earlier that day in Ireland, I can tell you. It was like stepping into another universe.

But nonetheless, wherever I go, I am always struck by the smile of a stranger. Not just the hint of a smile but the one where the whole face lights up, the eyes are alive and while it lasts, even for only a second, the beam has an eternal quality about it. The smiling person passes never to meet again but a rich exchange has taken place. This is a very basic form of communication. And I think Irish people do have an open, smiling sort of way that lets them connect easily with strangers. But the smile is also that they're genuinely interested in others, it's not just fake. And I think visitors really notice that when they go to Ireland. So I do think social rapport is easier for Irish people than for some other nationalities.

Not easy

'It's dead easy, emigrating to England', I said to my older brother when I was a young lad in Ireland. 'It isn't', he said. I always remember that. Because of course he knew something about it already, and I didn't. He had emigrated before me. And in fact, when I did go, those first ten years were incredibly hard. I remember going into a pool-hall here in England wanting a game, because I used to love playing pool. And we'd wait in line all night long but no matter how long we waited, we Irish could never get a game. It reminds me of those signs there used to be in pubs, lodgings, some shops even at that time: *No Spitting. No Dogs. No Irish.*

Richard Harris, the great Irish actor of stage and screen - when he first arrived in London, he saw for the first time in his life a sign like that. And do you know what he did? He put his hand straight through the glass, grasped the sign, took it and kept it! He kept it all his life, on display in his own house. Wasn't that wonderful? What a man. He didn't even *hesitate*!

Many Irish people came to England in those days just to work and make a bit of money, often hoping to return home again to settle. But I had to leave Ireland for political reasons, because I couldn't live there safely anymore at that time. It was the time of the *'Troubles'* in Northern Ireland. I got a bit politically active where I came from in the North and at one point my family realised I was about to be in really serious danger. I never committed any crime but you didn't have to, to be at risk of being kidnapped, kneecapped or interned. That night, my father told me to take the boat and get myself over to England, where I could 'disappear' for a while.

At that time, as is still the case now, there was free movement for Irish and British people between the two countries, so I was able to come here and 'disappear' into London. Although that wasn't easy either because it was the 1970's, with all the IRA bombings going on here too in England as part of the war in Northern Ireland. Anyway, I kept a very low profile for ten whole years here. You had to, because there were so many arrests, you know, of ordinary Irish people across England at that time - swooping arrests and raids on homes in the night, based on the slightest suspicion that you might be an IRA sympathiser or supporter, or know someone who was.

I remember going into a newsagent's here in Cambridge to buy the *Irish Independent* newspaper as usual. But there had been an IRA bombing that day in London and I found myself *whispering* my usual daily request for the newspaper. I realised I had become ashamed to voice out loud my request to buy the Irish newspaper they were selling. Ashamed for my accent to be heard out loud, and it felt really bad to realise that.

It's interesting to look back in time at the problems of racism in Britain, like we're looking back in this conversation at those of the 1960s, 70s and

80s… And then to look at current racial problems, and trying to imagine the future of them as well, looking ahead.

But you know, we immigrants have contributed so much to this country and to the city of Cambridge. Nurses, teachers, builders… Look at the NHS today, totally dependent on qualified medical immigrants as staff… The Irish navvies and the Caribbeans built the roads and railways for much of England. Back-breaking work, that was. I once thought of adapting Oscar Wilde's title and staging a play called *The Importance of Being Irish*, about the contribution Irish immigrants have made to English society.[21]

You know, all across the world, migrants are by definition the *survivors*. Look at the Poles recently, working on farms out in the Fenlands… They have to work *so* hard for so little, and yet it was more than they'd get in their own country. You have to arrive and make your way in a foreign country and culture and find work and a home and try to fit in and learn a different way of life. It's well outside the *comfort zone*, you know? Something makes certain people just get up one morning in their own country and say '*That's it - I'm going!* I'm going to take the plunge and see if I can start all over again in a totally foreign place.' *Sink or swim…*

I remember a few decades ago, there was what was then commonly called a 'doss-house' at the edge of Cambridge. Irish labourers working to build the city's roads used to sleep there. And God, if you saw the conditions - the way they lived! It was like a bunker, crammed with little single beds and that was it. And they were so removed entirely from any other human interaction. They were away from their families back home. They had no women of any generation with them or around them. They were just workmen, all sleeping together in a shed. What an awful way to live. So dehumanising. And of course the building company and the doss-house between them probably had a special arrangement. The labourers sent some of their money straight home to keep the family in Ireland, and what was left they just drank for a bit of consolation before going back to the doss-house. And now thirty years later I see Eastern European workers

---

[21] Wilde's original title was *The Importance of Being Earnest*.

living in similar ways. Because in their eyes they're making good money, compared to what they could make back home.

Putting down roots

But despite all that, coming to live in England was also incredibly enriching for my life - there's no doubt about that. Incredibly enriching. In Cambridge at the beginning I remember meeting Cambridge undergraduates, who were so intelligent and well-educated, and they knew a lot about Irish literature. And that encouraged *me* to go to the library myself and get out Joyce and Yeats and Beckett and really discover them. I personally feel I was actually able to celebrate and develop my Irishness living here - more than I could ever have done where I came from in Ireland.

Because in some ways, from the minute I arrived here, I found the English very accepting. Compared to Irish culture at that time, they were very liberal and open, especially about sexuality and how you lived your private life. Being in England left me so much more room to develop my own individuality, to just be who I was at my own pace, than I would have had in Ireland. Back in Ireland before I left, someone had once said to me: *'The nice thing about you, Fionn, is that you do everything just a little bit differently. You're in the crowd, but not of the crowd...'*

But being Irish in England is of course very different from being Irish in other countries. As you know yourself, it's hard being Irish here, whereas in many other countries - in France, Germany, the USA - you're a hero if you're Irish. There, it's a very popular identity that's looked up to.

But between Ireland and England there's so, so much intense, negative history - colonisation, war, racism... And then within England, Cambridge in turn has a very particular atmosphere as well. Cambridge is quite 'rarefied', isn't it? So being Irish in Cambridge, your Irishness is surrounded by and viewed through this particular lens of what 'Cambridge' is as well...

But London, where I first arrived, was wonderful for me. For the first time in my life I had three months of unadulterated freedom! Then when I

144

moved to Cambridge - all that lovely architecture! And it was multicultural. There were green spaces. People were cultured and well-educated. Among ten Irish people you might meet in the Portland Arms pub in Cambridge, nine of them would have degrees.

There was, and still is, such a variety of people here - a mixture of people from all over the world. For instance I remember a Cambridge neighbour of mine, an elderly Russian lady who had migrated here. She loved chess and arguments! I felt I was surrounded by thoughtful, educated people. It's interesting that back then, most of the people I was surrounded by were males - my friends, colleagues, neighbours, companions. Whereas now that I'm older I find most of my friends are women. Making up for lost time, maybe!

I'm deeply attached to Cambridge now. I once had a moving experience in Little St Mary's Church here. It was a time when I was very low, after the break-up of my marriage. I went in there and for some reason I opened the big Bible on the lectern, thinking: 'I need something out of this - I feel so low'. And the page I happened to open said: *This is my Beloved Son in whom I am well-pleased...* Glancing around first to make sure there was no-one there, I slammed it shut and shouted out angrily: 'No-one's bloody well ever said that to *me...!*'

And years later when I told this story to someone they said to me, 'But Fionn, don't you see that that day - there and then in Little St. Mary's when you opened the book and asked for a response, it *was* said to you right then?' And it hadn't dawned on me at the time! So Little St Mary's and its wildflower garden right in the heart of the city next to the Guild Hall, that's a very special place for me.

I was impressed by my ex-wife who, after we separated, just easily uprooted and took herself off to Scotland. Just up and off. But I feel so rooted here, I'd find that very hard to do, to just leave Cambridge like that now. And I do feel very appreciated by my immediate neighbours here in my street. They know I'm there to help them if they have any difficulty, and that I genuinely care about them and their welfare. They see that, and they come to me and appreciate me being around. As a council tenant I was able to get involved with policies that impinged on the lives of my neighbours. A friend pointed out to me that I was in a position to help them over some proposals that the Council had floated. So I organised the neighbours and we were able to contend with the Council and reach a very acceptable outcome. I remember saying at the time, 'It was achieved without spilling a drop of blood!' Instead during the whole process there were many smiles, because a smile will predispose a person to listen.

But what is it that makes one person stand out as the neighbour that others know they can go to, who'll do things for them and always help? I think it's *joie de vivre*. Being open and approachable. And having a certain amount of energy and strength of character, to persist and make those phone calls to get things done to look after the environment and everyone's quality of life. And above all, maybe that ability to smile: the smile of a stranger is a wonderful thing, isn't it? It's the best thing of all.

I'd probably like to live here now for the rest of my life. This is a social housing complex designed especially for older people and it's gorgeous. The garden is beautiful, the quality of the materials throughout the buildings and courtyards, the flow of light, the mix of privacy and community... It's been very carefully created. And the warden is a woman who goes way beyond the call of duty for her residents. We have several nice communal spaces. There's one where I help organise play-readings and performances, and another where we can go line-dancing every week.

But I went to a residents' meeting yesterday at another housing scheme in the city for elderly English residents and I must say I came away from it feeling really depressed. The tenants seemed so lifeless and closed in on themselves - a bit bitter and with no wider interests or appreciation of life. Maybe I'm being harsh but I went away really asking myself: 'Does old age have to be like that?' I know society has difficulty relating well to senior citizens - but seeing them yesterday made me understand why! It's a two-way thing, isn't it? And yet each of those people I suppose has their own rich story, if only we could access it.

Challenging racism

Of course there's anti-Irish racism and stereotypes among the English, but overall I feel that, although it's been hard, being Irish in England has worked greatly in my favour - really greatly so. People have this preconception of Irish people as being friendly, cheerful, open, approachable… That's worked well for me, so long as I've been able to manipulate it to my advantage (laughs). But if someone says to me *'Oh you must drink a lot too'* - I have to put them right on that. Or if they call me *'Paddy'*, I'll object to it instantly. I don't want to be called a *'Paddy'*, because it was always meant to be disparaging, to mean you were lesser than an English person.

But I must admit I sometimes also play up to the idea of being 'Irish' - it's a great way of getting attention in England, whereas of course back in Ireland you'd be no novelty! Although it worries me a bit sometimes that I do that! But there's no doubt that in one way or another I've celebrated my Irishness ever since I've been in this country.

You know I was head of admin for years at one of the colleges here in Cambridge. People felt I did my duties well. But once I had a conflict with this one senior colleague, where I just couldn't get him to cooperate or provide a certain bit of work that was needed. I couldn't figure it out. And eventually another senior colleague came to me and explained, quite kindly: *'Fionn, don't you see? The problem is just your Irish accent. I'm afraid he's a racist.'* I was dumbfounded. He explained: *'He'll always just dismiss anything that comes from someone with an Irish accent - you know, as not being serious, authoritative, important or whatever…'*

But in fact that man who felt that way about Irish accents, he was just an ignorant man overall, a very difficult person. Another time, we were disagreeing over some point of work and he said: *'I'm taking such and such a position whether you like it or not, and if don't like it you've every right to say 'Bollocks' to me.'* And I said, *'That's your language, not mine. And I walked away.'* Which made him furious, I think.

I was always very concerned not to allow those sorts of English people to view me as an inferior being, like they tried to do. That they not be allowed to get away with thinking I was a thick, stupid Irishman, or that all Irish people were backward. Because there used to be, at least, this perception in Britain of the stereotypical ignorant 'Paddy'. Think of those racist English cartoons in 'Punch' magazine portraying the Irish as always fighting, drunk and with very big families. And remember that up until the mid-1980's Ireland was still classed by the World Health Organisation as a Third World economy.

So when I was a bus conductor I would stand on the buses whistling classical music to myself. Or I'd speak a bit of French to French tourists on my buses. Or I'd read some big classical tome of a book on my bus, holding it under my arm while I worked.

It's true that as Catholics, my wife and I weren't practising birth control. But I couldn't tell anyone we were expecting another child - I just couldn't! I felt too ashamed. And it was only our third child! But I thought people would talk about us, y'know, saying 'Oh those Irish, they can't control themselves, they all have these huge families...' and so on.

But what native English person actually knows *what it's like* to be an immigrant? Plucked from your home environment and dropped into another country, trying to build a life there... The fundamental thing about English people is that they've never, in the modern era, been invaded and colonised as a nation. They have no idea what that's like - the damaging effects it has on a nation for decades and generations. That's what I always ask myself too, in any given situation: *what do I really know* of what it's really like for someone else? The analogy for this in my mind is always: no young person can know what it's really like to get old. You can think about it, but you don't know what it's like.

Even when they go abroad, you can see that English people tend to be unconsciously locked into experiencing things from that English viewpoint - that of a huge colonial invader and power, up until recently. That's why they often have that terrible reputation abroad - as being boorish and arrogant, ethnocentric, unwilling to learn others' languages and cultures and so on.

And then it's especially hard to come in as a migrant to the very country that has invaded and colonised your own country, and hence has a colonisers' view of your people... And then, among all migrants, those coming in as political asylum-seekers and refugees are at a totally different level of difficulty again. For instance, the other day I met a young woman from the Ivory Coast at some event - a beautiful, bright young woman - and I had a long chat with her. She was lovely. I only found out afterwards that she has asylum here because she had undergone torture over there. Just imagine it: *torture*! Just really imagine it. I just couldn't believe it or stomach it. Such a beautiful young woman.

You know there are all these things that were a huge part of the Irish experience for decades, for centuries. Being colonised by military force, having your language suppressed by the colonisers, being displaced, having to emigrate, suffering racism. And although we need to remember our history, it *is* history hopefully. You'd hope all that is entirely in the past now - and it mostly *is* for Irish people. But what's shocking is to see how so much of this is happening right now in the present again for other peoples.

It's as if it goes in cycles: now it's the Middle Eastern people who have all this trouble here in England because a tiny minority of Middle Easterners set bombs. That was the same for Irish people during the IRA campaigns. And these problems are only beginning for whole waves of other people now - like for the Eastern Europeans and Romanians who are coming in now as migrants to Ireland now, and suffering racism there today from some of the native Irish.

Outside the comfort zone

I feel that people who stay living in their own country all their life, no matter what that life is, still live inside a certain permanent sort of comfort zone. You've never really stepped outside your comfort zone till you've gone to try to start a new life from scratch in a foreign country. In the bible, the writer of the Psalms captures what it's like to be an exile. I'll recite it for you:

By the waters of Babylon,

there we sat and wept,

remembering Zion.

On the poplars that grew there

we hung up our harps,

for it was there that they asked us - our captors -

for songs, - our oppressors -

for joy.

'Sing to us' they said,

'one of Zion's songs'.

But how could we sing

the song of the Lord

on alien soil?

Can an exile ever be happy on foreign soil? That sense of feeling homesick is beautifully detailed in the book *The Wind in the Willows,* when Mole begins to miss his home, and the author talks about home being an anchor in one's life. And if, what's more, you are going to live in a country that has negative stereotypes about your own nationality - well then you'll really be outside your comfort zone trying to make your life there, I'll tell you that much! Over the years, fortunately, I achieved a sense of contentedness, but I feel that I will always have one foot in Ireland. When you look back on emigrating, you're glad you did it, but it's really tough at the time.

But for instance when I retired after my working life here in Cambridge, instead of putting my feet up quietly, I suddenly decided to step *way* outside my comfort zone again by doing an ancient 700-mile walking pilgrimage down through France! It's called the Santiago de

Compostella pilgrimage - down through France to Compostella in northern Spain. That's madness - sheer madness, isn't it? Hundreds of thousands of solitary walkers have done it before me since the early Middle Ages, but for every single one of them it must be a kind of inspired madness, mustn't it, that makes them get up from their everyday life and strike out and say '*I'm off! I'm going! For no good reason at all I'm just going to head off and take a leap in the dark and walk the Compostella pilgrimage and see what happens to me along the way...*' God just inspires us to branch out like that, doesn't he, and see what happens! Like Laurie Lee in his book *As I walked out one midsummer morning* - he just had that urge to just get up and go.

And that Santiago pilgrimage was a really, really tough adventure for me. I was often lonely, lost, depressed, exhausted, and wondered what the hell I was doing there. But it was also marvellous - of course I wouldn't undo it now for the world. A few years ago I wrote a book about the experience, called *Alone to Compostella*. I took it to a printer in Cambridge and got 100 copies printed and sold them all to friends and family.

Communicating

I've been listening to a series of radio programmes about the region Jesus lived in. They're setting his life back into its political context of the time, showing the political situation at the time in the neighbouring areas of Syria, Jordan, Palestine and so on. The programmes really show that it was ground-level people that Jesus was mixing with. They weren't cardinals, remote on their thrones in Rome! They were rough working people. And his communication touched them so they were *getting involved* with him at an absolutely ground level.

I always think that Jesus was a great communicator. The way he used metaphor. Like using the metaphors of sheep, and of fish. Sheep and fish were something the people around him knew all about. He was surrounded by rough-hewn, swarthy, stinking fisherman. They weren't thinkers or talkers. But he was able to take the images of things they knew so well, and turn them around to convey things they'd never thought about before. In a different environment and time, he'd have had to use different images, the metaphors of the time.

Recently I've been helping to publicise a staging of *The Importance of Being Earnest* by our Irish playwright Oscar Wilde. He was a *wonderful* communicator like that - so *focused* on exactly what was going on and what he was trying to convey. When I created the Cambridge Irish Culture Festival, it was as a response to the BNP, the racist, fascist British Nationalist Party that was popular back in the 80s. I wanted to do something cultural - something open and integrating - as an antidote to racism, the BNP and the ongoing war in Northern Ireland, as well as wars in other places.

It might sound strange, but in founding the festival, I felt I was somehow contributing to the Peace Movement in Northern Ireland. I was trying to reach out through theatre and the arts to show here in Cambridge a positive view of Irish culture and Irish people - one that wasn't violent, wasn't negative, that was creative and open…

For instance I remember when I was a student in Ireland, in one place in the school I saw that the loos were in a terrible state. So I just set to straight away to clean them! The pans were all stained. So I used to lock up one of them each day and set to work on it until I'd worked my way through cleaning them all. I just saw it needed doing and did it. That's the way I was raised at home.

I remember too that as a youngster I went straight into a GCSE-level French class and hadn't had the years of French the others had. But straight away I took to the language and just did lots of extra evening work on it off my own bat, in my own time, out of interest. The others used to give me a mocking for that, but I just had to carry on regardless and plough my own furrow. Fortunately the teacher was an encouraging sort of person who nurtured my studies. Now even to this day I love the French language, speaking it, writing it, even though I get things wrong.

That's the way I was raised in Dublin by my mother. There was no welfare state for anyone in those days. And around the house if something needed doing, she had that expectation that one of us would step up straight away and just do it.

It's like the guy who founded the Cambridge Folk Festival back in the 1960s. Ken Woollard was his name. I knew him because I used to do a bit of folk-singing at a folk-music club in town. One evening I remember he came in and said: 'Guys, we should get something going here, something a bit more organised for folk singers...' Well he mobilised a few others and they started a group of singers at Cherry Hinton Hall. And believe it or not that's where the huge, world-famous Cambridge Folk Music Festival came from. This behaviour is the opposite of that *'Don't get involved'* attitude, which I suppose you can get anywhere. That culture of *'Keep your head down - just work 9 to 5* (or not, as the case may be!) *and stay away from anything else...'*

You know, people will queue for days on end to vote in the first elections they ever have in a country. But then it gets so difficult, doesn't it, to stir us all out of our apathy later on. We live in a welfare state and so many people think 'Oh the state will look after everything for us.' I feel that kind of excessive dependence robs you of something as a person: creativity, drive, intellectual curiosity... The welfare state is excellent in many ways but there is that downside. But I suppose there'll always be people who'll over-depend on the system, who for whatever reason just can't or won't step outside their comfort zone. For instance, I know someone who sits in her council house in front of the telly 13 hours a day, smoking. She does nothing else, sees no-one, seems to want nothing more.

I think of a verse from *The Psalm of Life* by Longfellow:

> Let us, then, be up and doing,
>
> with a heart for any fate;
>
> still achieving, still pursuing,
>
> learn to labour and to wait.

I first read this poem as a thirteen-year-old and even then I was impressed by it. By whatever good fortune I have been imbued from my youngest days with this urge to *'Be up and doing...'*

But the best statement I've ever heard about community is by the medieval monk St Bernard of Clairvaux, who said community is all about 'the enhancement of the individual'. I really agree with that. In a true community you don't have to lose your individuality - you can become even more your unique self by living in communication with others and contributing to the community.

 Political violence, religious repression, covert and overt racism, sexual liberation, ethnic pride, the joy of anonymity in a liberal foreign country... It's all there, plastered across Fionn's life history.

And the hunger of a working-class boy for education. Fionn is a natural, life-long autodidact who had never accepted the implicit rule that only upper-middle class people should *produce* high culture - that is, write books, direct plays, organise festivals, as he has done. I'm not sure he had ever noticed this rule in the first place.

This reminded me of when I returned to Ireland from France to spend a couple of years as a young lecturer at the National University of Ireland, before coming to work in Cambridge. In Ireland I was struck by the incredibly high proportion of the ordinary working population who wrote books, ran theatre companies, wrote for newspapers, showed their art in exhibitions and performed concerts. These young intellectuals were all from what here in Cambridge would be considered very working-class backgrounds. And they were often unemployed or on very low incomes while they did it.

But it seemed to be the natural thing to do - routine self-expression - for that generation who grew up while Ireland was starting to liberalise in the late 80s, and had free university education that was of a world-class standard. On arriving in Cambridge later, I was amazed at the difference - how the upper and upper-middle classes here seemed to have an iron grip on the right to produce culture, and how docile the rest of the population were about letting them get on with it.

There are some odd paradoxes in the relative haven that England offered in the 70s and 80s for refugees from the war in Northern Ireland, like Fionn. Oddly, all through the three decades of the war in Northern Ireland, the mutual 'open door' policy for migration between England and Ireland never altered. England remained the place where Irish people on either side of the war in Northern Ireland could disappear to, for a while or forever, if in immediate danger of internment, kidnapping, beatings, execution or the dreaded 'kneecapping'. I have always wondered why England left this door of self-service asylum open to Irish people during the war, while also arranging such enormous measures for the surveillance, interrogation and internment of the Irish migrant population in England once they got here.

The boat to England was also the inevitable route for any couples formed across the great divide that the war was all about - where one partner came from the population who wanted a decolonised United Ireland, and the other from the group who wanted to stay part of the British Empire. Such couples couldn't stay alive in Northern Ireland at that time, and had to flee abroad.

But as a thread running through Fionn's story, it's clear too that coming to live in the country that colonised your own country adds particular layers of challenge to the migrant experience. Of course the great majority of migrants in England are in that position. The reason that Indians, Pakistanis, Bangladeshis, Kenyans, Zimbabweans and Jamaicans were allowed to flock to England for a time from the 1950s onwards was precisely because they were from former British colonies (almost as if it was pay-back time).

But compared to those other peoples, Irish people seem to hold a much more damning, unambivalent memory of how the English behaved as invaders in their country. When I have asked Indians or Africans about this, they are usually more ambivalent. They often cite some advantages brought by the English invasion of their country, rather than just condemning it outright. I've never heard an Irish person take that pro-colonial perspective.

Like most frictions, the feeling is mutual. Around certain specific migrant groups like the Algerians in France or the Irish in England, the hosts - understandably - reserve a half-conscious memory of the bloody wars of independence with which that colonised nation kicked them out. This tension is heated further when decolonising wars drag on, as the one in Northern Ireland did into the 1990s.

But perhaps having a historically racist view of a people one has colonised is inevitable. To invade another nation, claim its lands, enslave its people, suppress their language and carry away their food and produce to your own country leaving them in famine, you must first represent them to yourself as being lesser than you - as somehow deserving this treatment - if you want to maintain to yourself and others a positive self-image as a civilised nation. It's clear from the popular press in nineteenth century England that the strategic forms of racism that gave this *permission* were an important component of Britain's colonial occupation of Ireland and other countries. [22] This kind of 'strategic' racism helped invaders like the British to maintain a positive self-image around their own drive to invade and conquer 'empire' - whereas for instance the Nazis' invasions to conquer *their* 'empire' were universally abhorred.

Like Saoirse, I had noticed how here in England you are expected to live as if that warring past didn't exist, and to just get on with *now*. After many years of resenting being pressed to think that way, I can now see that it is a pragmatic strategy that can more or less work. It enables you to get on with your life in the present, to live among and forgive those who have done your people wrong in the past (even when they don't concede they've done anything wrong), and to appreciate the various good things that they do for you and others in the present.

---

22 Pseudo-science classifying Irish people as sub-human primates was the norm even in educated English society right up to the late nineteenth century. It strategically buttressed and 'justified' the continued occupation of Ireland. As recently as 1860, the Professor of Modern History at Cambridge University wrote about Irish people, in all seriousness: *'I am haunted by the human chimpanzees I saw in Ireland. (...) I don't believe they are our fault. (...) But to see white chimpanzees is dreadful. If they were black, one would not feel it so much.'*

This charmer - one Professor Charles Kingsley - was a highly respected academic, and a national thinker. He is quoted in *Anglo-Saxons and Celts - A Study of Anti-Irish Prejudice in Victorian England* by I.P. Curtis, New York University Press, 1968, p.84.

Chapter 9

Stefan

From a Nazi camp in occupied Poland

If people could see those things, there would never again be war
Polish saying

 Stefan's bungalow is immaculate in that way that his World War Two generation have, of having everything just so and in its place. They knew the era before mass-consumerism. Possessions were bought gradually with frugal savings, long before the days of credit for everyone. June, his wife, is trim and sprightly in her eighties. Her hair is neatly permed. She's wearing pearls over a smart cashmere sweater. Stefan shows me into the sitting-room and seats me with an old-world, courtly hospitality.

On a low table between us, little dishes offer olives, nuts, gherkins, salami. He pours me some wine. I comment on the beautiful glasses, which I notice are made of very fine crystal. He says they are from near his home in Poland, where they specialise in crystal. When his back is turned I flick the glass discreetly with my fingernail and it does indeed sing back that high, sweet note that only the finest crystal can emit.

When I casually taste the wine, I am taken aback to find it is extraordinarily - extravagantly - good. I say so. (It's better than any I tasted at High Table in my College, despite our famous wine-cellar.) He explains that he's a member of a national wine club who send him fine wines by courier. Sitting down at last with a sigh of relief, he says it's supposed to be good for the heart.

A heavy-set, corpulent man, he has an air of settled, natural dignity about him. When he sits, he is as upright in the chair as an athlete, his big weight settling around him. There is an air of decency about him that anyone would notice. In this he reminds me of Ruth, my first interviewee, who came from starving Africa. These are people who, in any setting, stand out for their calm, unhurried warmth, their sheer presence.

It is striking that Ruth and Stefan are also the two in this book who have done the lengthiest, most back-breaking, demeaning physical labour. Yet rather than being broken by it, they both have the physical grace and dignity of friendly kings.

The way Stefan welcomes me in, I get the sense that inviting guests in to enjoy the goodness of his household is a cornerstone of human interaction for him - a cultural foundation that he brought with him from some time and place far away, long ago. Something he *chose* not to let go of, despite his exile in England.

The seriously good wine; the continental finger-food to go with it because it's the hour of the *apéritif* on the continent; the calm, regal bearing as he sits waiting for me to savour the tastes before we talk... This is not what I was expecting from a 90-year-old who spent his entire working life down the English coal-mines.

Decidedly, there is more than meets the eye to this Stefan. You can feel that he trails behind him almost a century of deeply *European* history, and that he decided to bring it all along with him - not to let it go - when he was forced to drop everything else.

Stefan

The effects of war

There are a lot of young Polish people coming to England now over the past few years just to work. They make a good name for themselves and are known as very hard workers. They're well-educated. And most of them are here out of choice just to earn some money, and then they'll go back home to Poland fairly soon.

But things are very different for them now than they were for us when me and my friends had to come here at the end of World War Two. We didn't have many choices then, I can tell you!

I was born in Bydgoszcz in northern Poland where my grandfather was a fruit-farmer, growing orchards and harvesting fruit for jam-production. He also had big ponds where he bred carp for sale. The Second World War broke out when I was 14 and it changed the course of my life forever. The things that happened to me during the war led to my having to leave Poland and make my life here in England, and being here talking to you today.

I was 16 when my father was captured by the Russians and thrown into a prison-camp in Siberia, where he was executed. Within a few years I myself was taken into German forced labour camps, then taken prisoner of war and moved around Germany, Italy and France before finally being liberated by the Allies towards the end of the war. They brought us Polish prisoners here to England because the English badly wanted foreign labourers to work in the mines. So that's what we did.

I am happy that my story is being told here because all the terrible things that happened to people in those days deserve to be recorded and told. All through my life, later, I've always tried to keep reading a lot of books about the history and politics of the Second World War. I was always, always reading, just to try to really figure out and understand the things that happened to millions of us in those years - to so many ordinary people all across Poland, Germany, France, England... Things that affected us forever afterwards. That's what really interests me - to try to look back and understand it all. What was going on behind the scenes. All the decisions taken by politicians and the heads of armies, that had such huge effects on millions of ordinary people's lives...

I feel it's still affecting us even now. I'm 90 now but I'm still always thinking about it all. Trying to figure it out, wondering how things could have been different, if things had taken a different turn. I think about my own life too. How would my life have been different if those first incidents that took me away from Poland hadn't happened? Or if I'd been taken to the United States after being liberated by the Allies, instead of being brought here to England? Or if I'd been able to go to Australia?

I still stay very much in touch with my family in Poland. My sister-in-law, Ulla, who is an old friend, used to come over to England to stay with us for a long holiday every few years. She has all the same memories I have from that time, when first the Russians and then the Gestapo came into our area in Poland. Sometimes we talk a bit about the memories and the things that happened back then, and how they affected us all.

The Gestapo came rolling into our town in their lorries. They came into the houses and took out a range of the men and boys at gun-point and rounded them up onto the town square. They then shot them down in a row with machine-guns in cold blood along the town square. They just murdered them in cold blood in a row in the town square in front of everyone. I saw that happen. That's how they used to get total control over the people. That would be their first act and after that they knew they were in total control - first after killing off so many of the men in the town, and then also because they had everyone afraid after that, so they had total control. That was their way, those Nazis at that time.

That was what they did to our own local Polish people. But then soon they also started bringing in Jews in lorries from elsewhere, into our town. They'd take them up to the hill outside the town and make them dig their own big mass-graves. Then they'd line them up and they'd machine-gun them along in a line straight down into the mass-graves. Then they'd just pour the earth in on top of them directly. You'd hear the machine-guns from the town-centre.

People said there were up to 65,000 Jews disposed of up there by the Nazis in that way. My young Polish friends in the town used to say among themselves that if you went up to that hill at night and looked at the mass-graves a few hours later during the night, you could see the earth still moving. I don't know if it's true. I never went up there to look.

Around the very start of the war the Russians also came rolling in to our town. They also rounded up a number of the men-folk and took them away. They came and took my father in that way, and we never saw him again. We found out later that he had ended up in a *Gulag*, a Russian labour camp in Siberia. He was there for a few years. And I'll tell you how it happened that he died there. We the family heard about it some months after it had happened - the Russians sent an official letter to my mother, telling her.

What happened in the Siberian *Gulag* was that springtime came. And in spring a bit of sunshine came to that horrible, freezing place. The prisoners were in a camp surrounded by barbed war. But this particular day in spring the sun shone brightly for the first time that year, and a few of the men lay down on the grass to feel the bit of sun on their faces.

Of course they shouldn't have done that. They knew that the Siberian permafrost was still frozen solid in the earth just under the surface of the grass. But they just couldn't resist lying down on the new grass to get the first bit of sun on their faces.

And that's how my father caught a serious fever. But it wasn't the fever itself that killed him. When he had the fever he became totally delirious, and in his delirium he just walked straight towards the perimeter wires as if he was trying to escape. He just kept heading on out towards the fence, even after the guards called out to him to stop. And so they shot him. And many months later my mother received an official letter from the Russians, telling us he was dead. That was how my father died.

The missing watch

My grandfather had a fine farm, with orchards for producing fruit and jam on a large scale. I was always very interested in horticulture – all my life I've been growing things and seeing how they grow and what's the best ways to grow them - what they need, you know. Well it was agreed with my grandfather that I would take over the farm after I had been to college to study horticulture. But the war came and prevented all that.

What happened was that as a teenager, while the Nazis held Poland occupied, I was working for a while in a local orchard. A number of young people were working there. It was a local orchard but it happened to be owned by a German whose son I was friends with. One day they came over in a carriage and told me that from the following Monday I was to go to their smallholding where I was supposed to work in the orchard. The father of my friend also employed three girls who slept in the house and two girls who came in on a daily basis. The live-in girls slept in bedrooms but I had to sleep in a draughty corridor where I had to put my clothes in the gap under the outside door to keep out the snow. I went to work from 5 am to 7 pm in wet clothes. The food was not very good and I was only allowed to go home every fortnight from 2 to 4 pm to see my mother, have a wash and change my clothes.

But one day there was a big disturbance and everyone was in trouble because it turned out that a watch had disappeared from the landlord's house - and the German was determined to find out who took it and to get the watch back. I knew nothing about it until he started going around to everyone looking for his missing watch. Then he called in the German Gestapo who were patrolling our area, to show he was really serious about finding the watch and finding out who took it. As he was looking more and more from all the workers for this missing watch, one of the girls working there, a local girl, told him that she had seen *me* go into the room! She claimed that I had stolen the watch!

The German came and took me into his house and I remember my mother was there in the room too. I was 17. He had me standing in front of him and he was trying to get me to say that I had taken the watch - and to tell him where it was and give it back to him. But I couldn't! Because I didn't know anything about it. I couldn't tell him because I didn't know anything about that watch or where it was, but he thought I must know and just wasn't saying. I remember him hitting me blows across the side of my head and I fell down. He knocked me out more or less with blows to the side of my head, but I just couldn't give any information about the watch, and he wanted it back.

I insisted that I had not taken the watch so I could not return it. After three days he told my mother to come and the Gestapo arrived. I had to kneel down in front of the Gestapo and when I told them again that I had not taken the watch he hit me, asked me again and when he hit me once more, he knocked out two of my teeth. I remember that he knocked me out the third time and I fell unconscious on the floor. When I came round I saw my mother crying. The German said that the Gestapo now had been given my name: if I didn't give them the watch and say I had stolen it, I was going straight to the Nazi concentration camp nearby at Krakow.

My mother couldn't do anything right then but she went away and took some actions. She went to see the Mayor of our town because she knew that he had had a lot of respect for my father and he felt my father was a good man. The Mayor was thinking hard about it but he knew well what the Germans were like and he said to my mother no - there's going to be no way out of this for him. He'll be sent straight to Krakow now, unless I can convince the Gestapo to take him as forced labour instead for the labour camps in Germany, even though he's young. That's the only hope now, if I can convince them to do it.

And he did. The Mayor managed to persuade them to take me away to the labour camps rather than being sent to the concentration camp for this 'crime' I didn't do - of supposedly stealing the German's watch. So that's how I was taken away from my home in Poland. I was 17 years old.

Used as human shields

There were thousands of workers at the German camp I was taken to. We were lined up at 7 am and the Germans came and selected workers for various jobs on farms, cleaning stables out, whatever was needed, and took us on tractors and lorries to work until 8 pm. A few months later we were all assembled and about 120 names, including mine, were read out. We were taken to the train station the following day, and travelled all that day and night. On the following morning the train was sabotaged by partisans as we were near the French border. So we Polish prisoners had to stay there nearly three days without food, only with water from nearby streams.

Then we carried on to Chambéry in France. There was a big German army camp there, and we were put to work as forced labour, extending their training trenches. When it was done, troops used them for training purposes. We had been in our civilian clothes but now we we were made to wear old German uniforms from the First World War and our own clothes were burned to stop us escaping.

The Germans also developed a very nasty system to use whenever they opened up new front-lines in battle. Whenever they were taking a new town or frontier, we prisoner-labourers were made to wear those old German uniforms and forced to march in there ahead of the German army, so that the enemy would think we were German soldiers. If anyone refused to do it, they were just shot on the spot.

That way their enemies thought the Germans had more soldiers than they really had. And all those men at the front - the Polish prisoners dressed up in old German uniforms - would be gunned down straight away, long before any of the Germans themselves would be hit way back behind them. So they would use us prisoners as human cannon-fodder to get into new towns this way and push back the battle-lines of the enemy.

We ended up being for a time in France, in Grenoble. I picked up a bit of French there. We were also made to work on improving the path up to the top of the mountain at Chambéry, because a lot of French partisans were hiding there. Sometimes we were made to carry old rifles from the

First World War with five dummy bullets each (obviously they wouldn't give us live ones!). And when we saw partisans, we had to fire just to make a noise to alert the Germans. The Germans could then see where the partisans were and pursue them. We were used as bait in that way by the Germans, and many of us prisoners were wounded or killed by the partisans in the middle of those battles, as we were standing in the middle unarmed, wearing those old German uniforms.

It just happened that I was one of the survivors of all this and after a few months, the 60 or 70 of us who survived were sent to Italy, not far from Monte Cassino. I learned a bit of Italian too, while we were there. You needed to be able to speak a bit of the language wherever you were, like for trying to trade with local guys for a cigarette or some food. I already spoke German and Russian which I had learned at school back home in Poland, because we were taught those in school in Poland at that time. I didn't speak any English yet at that stage.

Monte Cassino was the Germans' staff headquarters and we had to do any jobs that were needed, including taking wagons containing rifles that were pulled by two cows, and sometimes even bringing back bodies to be buried. The Germans were cheats: the wagons were often covered with a white sheet painted with a Red Cross, as if they were carrying the wounded to hospital, when actually it was ammunition that was being carried in them.

When Monte Cassino surrendered, the German headquarters moved to a big mansion in Sasso Marconi. We were moved there to go up and take off the roof-tiles, to make it look derelict, although underneath nothing was actually destroyed - it was just an illusion. Then we were divided into different work groups. My task, together with a chap called Josef, was to take a small wagon loaded with empty batteries into Bologna for them to be recharged, as there was no electricity in Sasso Marconi, and to bring back fully charged batteries.

One day in that area, the Germans made me and my friends put on the old German uniforms again and be among the Polish prisoners marching ahead of them straight into a town they wanted to take. I thought I was definitely going to die that day, but it was actually in the middle of that battle that the war started to come to an end for me.

The battle started and my mates were being shot down all around me and I thought 'This is it'. My friend was next to me and I saw that he was just standing there rigid and paralysed. With the terrible noise and the fright of it and people being shot dead around us, he just froze and I could see his mind had just gone blank.

And I thought 'Well, we're definitely done for now - there's nothing for it anyway' so I just grabbed him and pulled him along with me and just ran for it. The bullets were flying everywhere. I dragged him along and pulled the two of us along a street and as far as a bridge nearby. There were bombs dropping now as well from an aerial bombardment directly overhead and we were sure to be killed by them unless I could get us down under the arches of that bridge. I managed to get us down there and we stopped there, hiding under the arches.

Eventually the battle calmed down and it turned out that the Allies had won it this time. And we were liberated! Me and my friend were down there huddled under the bridge for a few hours until eventually, Allied soldiers came along and found us. We went up to them and when we identified ourselves as Polish, the Canadians took us to their camp.

A Polish lorry then came and collected us and after interrogation, they put us in in Polish uniforms and gave us something to eat. It was the first time in a long time that we had some real food. We stayed there for a few months and then were taken to a place near Trieste where there was a huge prisoner-of-war camp holding the Germans who had surrendered in Italy. I was given the task of collecting food to feed them. I can't remember exactly how long for - six to twelve months.

Brought to England

When the war finally ended, we were put into the proper Polish army and were trained in Treia Maserata. After six months in training, I was selected to go to under-officers' school. However, a week before the presentation ceremony I went for a drink with a friend in Maserata. We were supposed to be back in camp for 10 pm, but as we were late my friend got a motorbike, managed to start it and persuaded me to ride on it as well. On the way back he tried to overtake an Italian wagon, but he hit a tree and we were thrown off into a field. My friend was killed. I suffered a serious head injury and was taken to hospital. I lost my memory. After a few days I was transferred to Barletta, which was the main hospital for the Polish army.

After several months there we were all loaded on to the Mauretania ocean liner in Naples, and sailed to Liverpool. The problem was that by the end of the Second World War, Poland was now occupied by the Soviet Union so they couldn't send us back home there. Returning from the west and having been liberated by the western Allies, the Soviets would just have sent us straight to their Siberian *Gulags*, like they did with my father, and we would have perished there like he did.

So we were all moved by boat to England. It took three days and I was horribly seasick for two days while we were in the Bay of Biscay. We were taken to a camp about twenty miles outside of Liverpool and for a whole week we were not given any food. We Poles were basically a sort of 'forgotten army', and we were refugees now due to the Soviet Union occupying our own country and being unwilling to let us back in. We ended up selling anything we could to buy food. Then supplies arrived and after another few days we were transferred to an ex-American army camp just outside Morpeth, not far from Newcastle. We spent two years in that camp because although Churchill wanted us Poles as a labour-force, the English trade unions would not agree to us working here.

While we were there, American officers came round to us and offered us passage to the US. Some people went to America. I thought I would go too but later I decided against it because I would have had to go and fight for them in the Korean War, which I didn't want to do. Once the English trade unions agreed to let us work where we were in England, we were given the choice to work either in the mines, in forestry or in farming. I chose mining just because it was the best paid, although the hardest.

I was claustrophobic and it took seven attempts before my friends could get hold of me and manage to push me into the 'cage' for the first time - the lift going down into the mines. After that first time I managed it better and got more used to it. So that was how I ended up in the English mines at the end of the Second World War.

The mines in England - oh, that was a hard life. All these Polish men who worked the mines for the English, they lived together in very hard conditions. Mostly just single men without any women or families. They had nothing to do but sit and drink or gamble or smoke cigarettes.

And working down the mines was *hard* work - dark, dirty, back-breaking work. I hated every minute of it, every day of my working life that I went down the mines, although the money could be quite good. I lived in Mansfield in a hostel which was filled with Northern Irish and Polish miners. My best friend there was Ted Pietrowski, and originally we both wanted to emigrate to Australia. We had our papers almost completed to attempt that. But I then met June, my wife, and after much deliberation I decided to stay in England and Ted went to Australia. He married an Australian girl. We saw them a few years ago when they came over to visit and we still write letters on a fairly regular basis.

Working in the mines, you were aching all over and really exhausted by the time you came back up. The health of so many miners was ruined by the mines. But the Coal Company's lawyers kept the cases going on so long that a lot of the miners who worked with me had died of their work-illnesses before they had to pay them out any compensation. I was 'lucky' in that I was medically retired early with lung-disease from the coal-dust, so at least I got my pension and have been able to enjoy my retirement.

I have lots of health problems now from the mines, but I try to ignore them. I'm nearly 90 now so I'm not doing badly. I keep exercising by working in the garden when I can. My son says that it's eating all the tomatoes that I grow that keeps me healthy! I'm also a member of a wine club and enjoy a glass of really good-quality red wine every day. It's good for the heart.

I remember that when I was living in that hostel like most of the miners around me, I used to play cards and gamble quite a lot. That was all we had for a social life, to relax you a bit after the week down the mine. But there was also the dance-halls. At that time young people used to go ball-room dancing. That was where they used to meet. They were huge dance-halls with hundreds and hundreds of people at them.

I wanted to be able to dance nicely so I went and took lots and lots of dancing-lessons. I spent a fortune at those lessons and I never could get anywhere with them. 'Relax! Relax!' the dancing teacher used to shout at me but I could never remember what to do with my feet, what way to turn and so on. The fox-trot, the polka, the waltz, the tango and so on. They were very difficult dances! I kept persevering anyway with the classes every week but I never did get any better at it.

The 'Nottingham Palais' was a big dance-hall where people used to go at the weekend and that was where I met my future wife, June. That was where a lot of men met their wives. I had dated a few girls in the area but when June and I started going out, it became serious quite fast. She was a young Englishwoman, and she had suffered a lot too during the war as a child and a young girl. Her grandparents were Russian Jews who had fled the pogroms against the Jews in Tsarist Russia, and migrated to join the big Russian-Jewish community in north London.

June's mother was divorced and hence a single mother before marrying June's step-father. With the step-father, they had to move around a lot in England during the war, and he was eventually killed in a light-airplane crash while June was still a young girl. June wasn't close to her mother at all, so I suppose like me she was ready to settle down with someone new and start a completely new life from scratch. It was when I met June that I stopped gambling and playing cards and straightened up. We decided to get married and we settled down in Mansfield, outside Nottingham.

First we rented a room, then got a council house. But we worked hard and fairly soon we were able to put a deposit down on a house of our own. We had two children, a girl and a boy. There was a big Polish community in Mansfield at that time, working in the Mansfield mines. And you had lots and lots of Polish friends around the town. We had The Polish Club where we occasionally went on Saturdays once the children were old enough. There the wives and the men would all socialise among themselves. There was a bar, and you could have Saturday lunch there. It was just full of Polish people. It only closed down in the 1990s. Up until then there was also always a good Polish deli in Mansfield, where you could buy good Polish foods from back home.

But the thing that bothers me most in England now is the 'yobbo' culture - violent English youth who don't work and have no respect for the law or other people. England wasn't like that before. Nowadays an older person doesn't dare to walk the streets in the evening. The yobbos even broke into my little walled garden at the back of the house just to steal my old gardening-tools. They'll literally take anything they can move.

Food in Polish culture

Good food has always been very important to me. Growing it, cooking it, eating and enjoying, sharing it with others... To Polish people, good food and hospitality have always been very, very important. Polish people really come together around food - as a family, as friends and neighbours. There is a big tradition of treating your guests very well. Also in my family there was a real tradition of growing, producing and preserving food. As I said, my grandfather had a horticulture farm and very big orchards, used for growing fruit for producing jam on a large scale.

Also my relatives in Poland have an old tradition of producing, potting and preserving lots and lots of foods in the home. Some years back when we went to visit them in Poland, they'd take us down into their cellar and it was a huge space with walls and walls lined with home-made preserves of every sort imaginable. Jars of fruit in syrup or in liqueurs - cherries, pears, peaches, raspberries and so on. And vegetables, meats, sauces, dried mushrooms - everything you could think of. They would either have grown them at home, or gone out into the woods to places they knew where they could pick them wild at the right season, to preserve them.

I kept up these traditions myself even here in England, whenever I could, and I hope I've passed some of them on to my own family. I always had an allotment and used to grow most of my family's fruits and vegetables. Actually there was often even more than we could eat - they say I have quite 'green fingers'! And I used to always take the family out into the countryside here to pick mushrooms. Not your common field mushrooms but the delicacies - what the French call *cèpes* and the Italian call *porcini*. They're really delicious if you know how to cook them properly. And I've always loved cooking, especially traditional Polish recipes like *Bígos* ('*Hunter's Stew*'), and dishes with wild mushrooms. My son is very much into cooking as well, and grows a lot of his own food. He's a medical scientist working on nutrition so he's carrying on the family traditions in his own way too.

Even since I had to give up the allotment, I still do as much gardening as I can here in my own back-garden. I still grow a lot of tomatoes in my little green-house every year. Ulla, that sister-in-law of mine from Poland, was here visiting a while back when my pear-tree was in fruit. She spent a whole day potting up the harvest of fresh pears in their own syrup. When my son came to visit he loved them, so I showed him the procedure for doing it. You have to do it very carefully, so they won't go off in their jars over time. So now Ulla's recipe for preserving home-grown pears in syrup has come over from Poland and been passed on here in England!

When Ulla was here last time, she also had a special message for me. Believe it or not, she had a message for me from that young girl who told the Germans she saw me steal the watch, when she knew I had nothing to do with it. She had died recently in her late 80s and before she died she asked to speak to Ulla. She asked Ulla to tell me that she was sorry, and to ask me to forgive her (which I did, of course). Apparently it had weighed

174

on her mind all those years, because she knew that it was her lie that had completely changed the course of my life and meant I couldn't live out my life in my own country.

As well as food and preserves, another big aspect of Polish culture that the older Polish men here kept up a lot was our love of chess. When my old Polish friends were still alive - mostly retired miners like me - we used to play chess non-stop. A few were still very much into politics - still believed in the Polish socialism of Lech Walesa, but I tried not to get involved in those discussions. When I play chess I like to make my moves quite quickly, but sometimes my friend used to drive me crazy, taking so long thinking about each move. I should get one of those timers! But once I played chess against a machine - a chess-computer that my son bought for me - and the bloody thing beat me!

In terms of nationalities, when my son got married it was a very nice wedding. The wedding party was less than 30 people in all - just both families and a few close friends of the couple. But there were six different nationalities, just among that many. There were English, Irish, Scottish, Polish, French and American! The wedding was held on the continent, the guests had travelled from four different countries, and half of them also lived in different countries from where they were born. It was nice to see people of so many nationalities, all getting on so well together around our extended family.

 Stefan is the only one of the interviewees who describes police beatings, although many of the others experienced them. Why that difference? Is it because he's so much older than them, and trying to put his whole life story into perspective now? Maybe, like the others, he wouldn't have discussed it when he was younger and was trying to put all that behind him and get on with making a new life?

Also, the Nazis are a sort of universal enemy, their regime and activities condemned by (almost) everyone of every nationality. Whereas interviewees may find it more complicated to tell about beatings by current governments. Iran, China, Ukraine, Zimbabwe, Israel, Sudan, Turkey, the British Army in Northern Ireland... I've interviewed people who have given accounts of being beaten by these and other states, but for all the reasons that the interviewees in this book have mentioned, these kinds of contemporary state violence by supposedly legitimate regimes are difficult and dangerous to discuss.

As in so many of the interviews, there is again here the theme of the intended education that was ripped away by the refugee experience, and becoming an autodidact in the new host country instead. Stefan taught himself to speak English, and then to read voraciously the great tomes of World War Two history that I see lining his book-shelves.

After the interview we go out to look at Stefan's garden. He has a real passion for plants, a passion transplanted to this little English garden from the flowering Polish orchards of his youth. The garden is colourfully immaculate, like a display at the Chelsea Flower Show.

He didn't get to go to horticultural college, or to inherit and run his fruit farm back home. That life was ripped away by circumstance - by one lie about a watch. But - like a little bud hidden from the Gestapo in the heel of his teenage fist - he transplanted the green gift.

Each of his plants here seems to have a little aura of vitality around it - crystalline and sparkling like his wine-glasses. His English-born son became a medical scientist specialised in plant biology. And at 90, Stefan shows me the new rose that he has just planted for next summer...

Chapter 10

Adar

From Kurdistan

A kind word warms a man through three winters
Saying from Adar's country

 Adar is about to be introduced to me by a bunch of his Kurdish and Turkish compatriots whom I already know from my outreach work for this project. They're extremely friendly guys. Easy-going taxi-drivers and takeaway workers, they really make a distinct effort to reach out and connect warmly with you. I presume that's part of their culture, as I've noticed they all have that same social behaviour.

A sort of floating presence hovering behind them now, Adar seems quite different. He's very tall. Broad-shouldered, well-dressed. Wearing a casually tailored jacket, he looks like a sociology lecturer or a political journalist. With his smouldering good looks, he glances down at me and looks away into the distance with indifference. I can't tell whether he means me to see and feel his indifference, like a pointed rebuff, or not.

I get the impression of a refined, highly educated man who is haughty and unreachable. I even have the fleeting, disconcerting sensation that he despises me on sight: a smug little White western woman who's getting a 'feel-good' factor from meddling in worlds of difficulty she cannot begin to know anything about.

Much later in time, when Adar has become a long-term personal friend, I will come to know that nothing about those first impressions I had of him was correct. They were all just projections from me onto the broad shoulders of that stranger, misreading his manner. As I got to know him and his life, I discovered that even in very extreme and painful circumstances, Adar never despises anyone. Instead, like a detective, he's always busy in that profound mind of his, searching - searching for the other person's perspective. When I get to know him much better, I will understand that no matter how distant an '*enemy*' the other may seem, no matter what that enemy is doing, Adar is trying to build up a picture in his mind of how things look from their side, and why they are doing what they are doing...

Adar

My background

I had to come here to England when I was 24 years old. Looking back, I feel now that I had been too active politically, at an age that was too young. That's basically the reason I ended up having to get political asylum here (even though I didn't speak a word of English at that time).

Being Kurdish, I come from a very, very fragmented background in terms of ethnicity, religion, nationality, politics, territory... I come from Turkey, but I'm not Turkish. I come from a Muslim country, but my area was not a setting where you could say conventional Muslim beliefs are held. And in the zone where I lived, to be politically active at all had been declared a criminal activity, whether you were involved in left-wing class politics or politics about ethnicity and territory. So when I was just 17 or 18 years old, long before I had to come to England, my life automatically consisted of sheer dissidence!

I was born in a Kurdish village in an eastern province predominantly made up of Turkish people. The town my family moved to when I was seven, mainly for educational reasons, was made up of a mixture of Turkish and Kurdish and Sunni Orthodox Muslims and non-Orthodox Muslims. All this made me think about identity - who I am. I always felt I had to protect my identity because it meant so much to me.

And as you know, this is a commonplace belief almost everywhere - that one must protect one's identity and stand up for one's beliefs and values. Anyway, if you come from a minority background, you do tend to stick together. You try to do everything in your own community and protect yourself from the mainstream ideas.

But now I realise that as a young person, I probably overdid it. I put so much emphasis on who I am, but at the expense of recognising others. Mind you, as someone from a minority identity, I wasn't welcomed either or allowed in to get to know those other people's differences. And I did try, just as I'm still trying here now in England twenty years later. But it's always hard to really get under the skin of another community who consider you an outsider, who consider you don't 'belong' with them.

So you have to learn their language, you have to learn a bit about the beliefs and the values that are held high there. And you have to familiarise yourself with the basic elements of their culture. But of course here in the British context for instance, there are some rules and conditions in their culture that I don't have any affinity with, that don't make me feel proud to live here.

In fact, language is one of the things I find most revealing about a people - it really reveals their collective values. I speak Turkish, Kurdish, German, English and some Arabic and French, so it gives me an overview of some very different languages. And I feel the mentality and character of the different nationalities is revealed so much in their languages.

I'm from a town in the south-east of Turkey, very close to the Syrian border. The border with Iraq is not far away either, further to the east. So I'm from the more Mediterranean and Middle Eastern end of the country. The other, more western end of Turkey has traditionally had a more European identity, whereas most of the country was considered to be part of Asia. This is part of the reason why Turkey's application to join the European Union was seen as problematic. Of course the whole country has always been a crossroads or buffer between Europe and the Middle East. But those borders have become constantly more sensitive now, with the highly volatile military situations in the Middle East.

I come from a farming background. I have my parents, four brothers and one sister, all still living closely in my hometown. I definitely miss them very much. It's quite difficult to be separated from them. Because actually, even though I'm a Kurd and I had to leave the country, I do like Turkey. I like the country and I like the people. I also feel a little bit sad about not having a strong Muslim identity because of the religious and spiritual context. I think religious views and beliefs are very important to all of us, really. They represent the spiritual side of humanity and we all desperately need that spiritual development, whatever religion we choose, in order to survive in this materialistic world.

As my first degree I did a political science degree in Turkey, at a very old university. I like political philosophy and at that time I read quite widely about European political theory - Jean-Jacques Rousseau, Thomas Hobbes, John Locke, Machiavelli, all those people… I wanted to get to know where western European thought was coming from. I read them all in Turkish, because I didn't speak any English before I came to England.

Then, circumstances led to my getting political asylum here in England. I had to learn English when I got here. Eventually, after nearly a decade I got British citizenship. I was very pleased to get my British nationality, because only then I was finally free to visit my country again to see my parents. I don't know if people realise that when you make an application for political asylum, it means you have to give up all connection with your country of origin and you can no longer cross its borders or return there. So you enter a sort of limbo or no-man's land, a kind of statelessness without any passport, while you wait to find out whether you can stay in the country you have applied to. So I was eight years in the UK before I could return to my country to see my parents.

My citizenship application process was particularly difficult because I applied for dual nationality rather than just asking to become a British citizen and to give up my old nationality completely. It's a much more difficult process, which is meant to encourage you to take the easier route and give up your old nationality. But I'm really glad I persisted and did it. Otherwise I could always have had problems in trying to get back into my country of origin to visit my parents who are still there.

Here in England I went on and did a Master's Degree in International Relations, and finally a PhD in political science. But I find Cambridge a very competitive place. It's a place where there are a lot of talented people who have a very high intelligence and a great reservoir of qualifications. If you are a refugee, or even just an English person in economic difficulties who needs any sort of job, you sometimes have to leave those qualifications behind you - just put them in a cupboard. The most common reason for refusal for several job applications I have done here was over-qualification, and I'm sure I am not the only one.

Relating to communities

Turkey is a very diverse country, although those who are 'proud to be Turkish' often don't acknowledge this great internal diversity in their country. But that's a problem everywhere, you know, people wanting to see a more homogenous community. Maybe they don't want to think about things in too complicated terms – they would like to keep simple minds. But in fact it is difficult for me to draw the boundaries of my background and where I stand within Turkey, within the country of my origin.

Within the Turkish-Kurdish community abroad, and here in Cambridge as well, there are a lot of divergent points of view about our own nationality and identities. There are practicing and non-practicing Muslims, people with modern and traditional points of view, people who support the Turkish government and people who are critical of it, people who defend the cause of the Kurds and people who don't, people who are well-educated and those with little education, people who integrate well into professional life here in England, and those who live in very isolated, difficult circumstances and have little integration. For instance, one of the Turkish community here said to me: '*That word* upsets people', meaning just the very term 'Kurdish'. Of course the word only upsets Turkish people who aren't themselves Kurdish!

But nonetheless, here in Cambridge, we in the Turkish community make a real effort to come together to support our community around the things we do all have in common, while staying tolerant of the differences among us.

You could say (with just a touch of exaggeration) that England is almost the opposite of what I said the situation in Turkey was. So here you do have all that acknowledged diversity that is there, but unacknowledged, in Turkey. But in England you don't have that community spirit that there is in Turkey. Well, in Britain the diversity is here and it is acknowledged. But it is brought up to you also as a barrier. Your identity and background are all acknowledged. But it is also to put you in your place in relation to British society. Addressing this diversity is done in a very managerial way. There is a gap between the bureaucratic way of managing the diversity, and the diversity as it is *lived*.

I think British society is having real problems assimilating or absorbing the degree of immigration and diversity here. The frame of mind of British society is just not able to create a world, a society, where English and newcomers can feel at home together, with a shared national identity. For instance, assimilation can be a valid way of coping with migration. That's done quite differently in some other parts of Europe. But in England the policy is closer to something like segregation. In a managerial way, you get to know things like the statistics of how many people there are within certain ethnical categories in the country. But they and the English people live separate lives.

I don't think English people's frame of mind can really accommodate the level of diversity that we have within the country today. For this reason they emphasise the bureaucratic management of diversity, but I'm not sure that's a real solution.

The whole discourse behind the level of refugees or asylum seekers coming into Britain, and the migration from Eastern Europe too, shows this is a problem. It's certainly not the only discourse, but it is the dominant one. What I mean is that 'Englishness' as an identity is not the type of host society that foreigners can assimilate into. As a foreigner you will never be invited to or expected to become 'English' - only English-born people can be English. Whereas in France for instance or in Sweden, there's a concept of national citizenship that foreigners are expected to join in with, to become truly French or Swedish themselves.

Because of the challenging difference between the world-views of the culture I come from and where I am now, I do feel out of place. Because of the indifference of English people and English culture, I do actually feel that I'm in exile - that I could never come to belong here, not least because English culture is so vague and fuzzy tht it's practically non-existent - there's nothing there to adopt or belong to!

Cambridge, for instance, has got a very diverse local community. And it would be really good to talk much more about what it's like to live in this truly interesting community. But unfortunately, we don't do that here in England, do we? You're supposed to just keep quiet and get on with life. We don't have the opportunity to cross over the boundaries of our own little worlds. We have some events about 'multi-culturalism'. We have certain small communication-groups that organise events, but that's it.

In the European context, the English and the French represent the two different models of citizenship. In France, because of their Republican tradition which English history has not known, you have a much more ambitious project of community. When you say 'I am French', this Frenchness means a certain set of shared citizen values. It is definitely very participative.

So I think I would feel much more at home in France. I don't feel my efforts towards trying to absorb 'Britishness' have been reciprocated. You go ten steps towards them, they will come one step towards you, but only as defined by the bureaucratic necessities. Yes, you have asylum but you also feel a little bit disoriented for the rest of your life here, and with a certain level of disorientation comes the feeling of exile.

 Apart from Hanh, the nine-year-old 'Boat Child' from Vietnam, Adar was the interviewee who had to seek asylum at the youngest age. In the early years, long before I met him, I know that he struggled to live here, in the sense that he struggled to live, full-stop. To like life enough to live it to his fullest potential.

Then, like a spider labouring up a very high wall, he set himself a very hard task and over many years, step by step, he completed it. Intellectually, he turned around to face back into the political and military chaos he had come out of, researching and writing a PhD thesis on the history, politics and struggles of the Kurdish people.

Then - again slowly and laboriously - he applied himself to climbing another wall by engaging his prodigious linguistic skills in qualifying as a Chartered Interpreter. Now he interprets between refugees and the Home Office officials who have to interrogate them to process their asylum-applications. It's skilled, hard, honest work that's decently paid and deeply meaningful. And there's plenty of it!

Now, every time he goes to work, the future direction of whole lives is hanging in the balance. He is trusted - formally and officially trusted, as if with a sacred duty - by both sides. Both sides trust him to relay their words in a fair and accurate way and they depend on him, because without him neither side can be sure of what the other has said.

For someone who has struggled to find meaning in his displaced existence and in the mundanities of careers, this job could hardly be more meaningful, not least because his role is to ferry back and forth the *true meaning*, which in this instance is a commodity more valuable than gold, as it will determine the whole future of a life.

He started his interview with me by explaining that growing up among Kurdish freedom-fighters made his existence automatically illicit. He was born into dissidence. The role he has now suits his nature better, I think. Like a sort of verbal Red Cross, he intervenes in the assessment interview to assist the asylum-seeker in their most vulnerable, critical hour. And to assist the English state with the hard task of deciding who is in *most* need of the scarce resource that is asylum (because they can't take everyone).

For someone who, at a tender age, experienced how violent official police 'interviews' can be in countries like his own, I think it's healing for him to have this intermediary, assisting role now in interviews that are similar - yet different. The outcome of each UK Home Office interview is always life-changing for that day's asylum-seeker, but at least the discussion is non-violent.

The dreaded police interrogations of brutal regimes, which so many of this book's speakers have known, rob the victim of any ability to tell their true story. In those physically painful conversations, your tormentors want words from you that you simply cannot give them. In Talya's case, they wanted the names of good people that she was not willing to hand over to them. From the 17-year-old Polish Stefan, the Gestapo wanted admission of guilt for something he had not done, and information he did not have but that they insisted they would get out of him.

By becoming a Chartered Interpreter, Adar has found a clever, socially beneficial way to repair that damage that was done to his own early experience of dialogue and conversation. The British asylum interview is a place where the refugee - like a wounded, broken bird, helpless, with nothing to offer - flaps in front of the great power that could save it. But even if that dominant power doesn't always take the broken bird in, at least they do no further violence to it. They have hired the gentle Adar to help construct, word by word, these life-changing conversations where every word matters and is officially, transparently recorded. With his trusted official role in those interviews, Adar is now able to contribute to this non-violence.

Today we're sitting in a Turkish restaurant that he's wanted to bring me to for a while. We both love Turkish restaurants. Me, for the delicious, healthy, copious Mediterranean foods and the delight with which they bring them to you, swinging each platter towards you with a flourish. He likes these places because they're a little fragment of the home country he loved -

a reprieve from the reserve and formality and tiny misunderstandings and accepted tensions of English life.

As if they were a sort of innocent Mafia, he knows every Turk and Kurd in town, and there are a lot of them. Insiders, brothers in asylum, they labour now over steaming trays of *kofta* and *kibbeh*, though most of them did very different things before. Swivelling the skewers over the naked flames, they inhale the aroma of hot frying onions, and dream for a moment of home.

Chapter 11

Kanwar

From Syria

Even a narrow place can contain a thousand friends

Saying from Kanwar's country

 *'Hi Marella, how are you?'* His greeting pops out cheerfully, though we've never met before. There's a summer heatwave on, and it's still hot at 8 pm. The work of the day is done: it's time to sit back, relax, connect. Everyone's melting placidly in the heat.

Probably in his late twenties, he could be a fitness instructor. He's tall, broad-shouldered, strapping even. Good-looking, with wrap-around black glasses. Dark tan, bright T-shirt, big white smile. Behind the glasses, I sense a gaze that is steady. Optimistic. I get the impression of someone who leaps forward to meet the world full-on, square-shouldered. Who permanently feels he has something to offer - right here and now - and gets stuck in.

But there is one profound difference between this man and all the speakers in the previous chapters. They sat in front of me in their homes in Cambridge. When they opened their doors to me I reached out and touched them, shook their hand. Tonight I'm sitting in my own house in Cambridge and yes, Kanwar has come to meet me here. But though I see an image of him in front of me, I can't touch him. He's a photo on a screen. And I won't even be hearing his voice tonight. Instead, his greeting spells out in type, unrolling slowly in front of me one letter at a time: *'H-i- - M-a-r-e-l-l-a...'* He is tapping it out laboriously on a little mobile phone that is almost two thousand miles from here.

At this moment Kanwar is sitting on the ground in the little tent he lives in with his wife and baby in the infamous refugee camp in Thessaloniki, Greece. He is 'with me' in Cambridge only through the miracle of technology. They are Syrian war-refugees, fleeing Damascus. It's July 2016 and they have already been on the road for four and a half years. They have survived in - and then fled from - refugee camps first in Kurdistan, then Iraq, then Turkey and now Greece. The 30,000 euros of savings that he took with him on this long odyssey are long gone, the last of it stolen by human traffickers who didn't even bother to traffic them. For some time now they have had nothing left in their possession except one change of clothes each and the mobile phone. Their child was born nine months ago in Domiz, the vast refugee camp in the Iraqi desert. Along with

50,000 others, their infinitesimally slow journey towards asylum in the west ground to a halt this spring against the newly-closed borders of Eastern Europe, where almost a million of their relatives and compatriots had filed through on muddy feet just a few months earlier.

Tonight this, my first encounter with Kanwar, will unfold through words that he is typing on his mobile phone in the Greek camp: I see them unfurl across my laptop screen in real-time in the same way as I am typing these words for you on this page now. He got my online contact details via fellow Syrians who had featured in the BBC documentary film *Exodus - Our journey to Europe*. They had won two of the very rare and coveted asylum-slots available in Britain. Professionals who speak flawless, humorous English, they're working in London now for humanitarian organisations and I am in touch with them. The BBC film conveyed what their lives had become since the Syrian war: jail, torture, beatings, broken bones, near-death experiences at the hands of human smugglers, near-drownings before being plucked from the open sea by coastguards... Through asylum, theirs have been relatively happy outcomes. But what in god's name to say now to this compatriot of theirs, who is locked out from the options that they ended up having?

Already in response to his cheery greeting, I'm lost for words. What the hell do you say? He's sitting in the mud waiting politely for you to type something back to him - and you're sitting in the comfort, peace and safety of your own home in Cambridge after a fine dinner.

I look about me. I'm relaxing on the couch in a beautiful glass extension that we added to our home. It juts out into the lush, enclosed haven of the garden, green and flowering. I'm an experienced writer but looking down at the blank screen, this moment feels surreal - like a hallucination. This is the most urgent, poignant, 'real-life' bit of writing I've ever been called upon to do and I have no idea what to type, to write, to say...

I type out: '*Hi Kanwar, it's really great to 'meet' you here like this on Facebook Messenger. I'm certainly fine here in Cambridge but how are you guys?! Do you two and the baby at least have a proper bed to sleep in, safely indoors?*' I don't know yet that they are living in a tent outdoors - I'll find that out later. He discreetly ignores the question for now and politely changes the subject by typing: *How is your work going?* This throws me completely - it seems madly incongruent. How can he be interested in my comfortable, middle-class work in Cambridge? But over the next ten minutes I realise that for this helpless, educated, professional guy with his perfect English, it's painfully valuable just to chat for a few minutes *as an equal* with any professional person who is active out there in any part of the free, normal, peace-time world. To talk about something else for a precious, alternative moment other than the mud, the cold, the hunger, the injuries, the humiliation, the thousands of desperate futures crowding in all around him.

I see that it is good for him to have someone out there in the normal world to chat with for a few minutes about higher things - one's writing, projects, cultural activities - like he and his friends used to chat about theirs on warm evenings at their favourite cafe in the square in Damascus before the war... That was what they knew. It's a future they hope to regain some day. And just to participate in it again for a moment with someone for whom it's the current reality is somehow (I will understand, much later) precious to him.

He types into his phone that he's glad my husband and I have had a nice dinner, and passes over my naively asking whether he has '...*at least had a decent dinner for the night?* It's going to take me a while to get the hang of conversing with this man in any way that's useful to him.

He tapped out his 'interview' on his mobile phone so that you could meet him first-hand...

Kanwar

How are you doing, Marella? How's your work going? Thank you for asking about us. Yes, we are stuck here in this refugee camp in Greece, living in a tent outside. In the camp it's very bad. I am helping a group of people by translating for them. They are Syrian and can't communicate with Greek-speakers or English-speakers. No-one is taking care of them so I'm doing my best to watch over them.

Our baby, Daniel, is nine months old. My wife delivered him in a *Médecins sans Frontières* clinic, back when we were in the Domiz Refugee Camp in Iraq. Here in Greece we are in very bad situation now - not enough food, and there are no charities or other organisations helping out here. The government doesn't really care about us refugees. Yesterday I had to go to a church to ask for some milk for the baby.

But I am a bit slow in writing these replies to you here this evening - forgive me. You're writing a lot to me, then I write just a little back! It's because it's a long time since I've done any writing, and also my phone is not good for typing into.

Thank you, sister, for your offer to post us some packages of things, but we can't have a postal address or receive any post here at the camp. I can't receive clothes anyway because I already don't know where to put the few things we have, as we only have a little tent to live in. I have just two sets of clothes for each of us, as there is no space in the tent for any more. Otherwise it's too difficult when we have to move, and we are moving all the time...

It's enough for me that you are trying to help. It means a lot to us. I will not ask anything from you. It's enough to have you as a friend. I don't want to bother anyone with me. And please say hi for me to your friends there in the UK who are working to help refugees.

[He logs off, typing...] Sorry, I must go now. I need to translate for a sick woman - a refugee here - who needs to go to the doctor. I will get back to you later...

[Later...] Hi, I'm back. You said that if I want, I could be like a 'reporter', sending you first-hand information about what life is like for people here in the Greek camps, and you'd get our experiences published in England? Thank you, dear sister, that's really cool. I agree - I will work with you to do it. All I have here is my little mobile phone but I can send reports to you on it, and photos, even videos ...

Do you want me to tell about my trip since I fled from Damascus with my family? Do you want it with details? Can I do it in several short stories, because there isn't enough space here on *Facebook Messager* to send you a long one? And can I send you some photos showing what life is like for people here in our camp in Greece? I will do it tomorrow. It will be with about 50 photos. Sorry about the quality of the photos - my phone is so bad. Sister, I am sending you our stories because I trust you. Some other people from the UK were not good with me before, so please don't forget this: I am trusting you.

So I am a 'writer' now - LOL! I promise to do my best. I've never worked for a newspaper and I've never been a reporter for TV. But I was a good reporter for *Médecins sans Frontières* and *Première Urgence - Aide Médicale Internationale* and other NGOs (non-governmental organisations), helping them with their goal of raising money for the refugees they were looking after. I will pray to God beforehand, then that will help me to not have any problems - LOL!

Anyway, so happy to have you as a friend online here. I am in a very bad situation but never mind, I will do my best to go on with you. I have nothing left but my friends now, so they are everything for me.

[The following evening, Kanwar pops onto my screen again in the Facebook Messager box, typing...] Ok, my story is ready. I will try to send it now... Is it ok? Did you receive it all? The last word on it should be '*hope*' - can you see it all...?

My journey

I'm a man in my twenties from the city of Damascus, the capital of Syria. I had specialised in English language studies and my original plan, before war broke out in Syria, was to found a humanitarian organisation or NGO. I used to work for the United Nations refugee agency (UNHCR) as a volunteer. Later, at the beginning of the war in Syria, with some friends we founded a humanitarian medical organisation to help refugees within Syria, who are known as 'Internally Displaced Persons'. I had also worked for an oil company as an English translator before I had to leave Syria.

Many Syrians want to be resettled in Europe because they think that there is no solution in the near future; others believe they have to stay in Syria because later peace will arise again. But about four and a half years ago, I and all my family decided we had to leave our home in Damascus - because staying in Syria meant death. Leaving illegally might also mean death, the only difference being that by leaving we were hoping we could find a way to survive.

For me, life in the war and as a refugee has been unimaginably difficult. In Syria I was arrested three times for speaking up for the Kurds - for their right to speak their own language, and other matters. I suffered a lot: they beat me and I spent a long time locked up in a place that looks like hell.

When we escaped initially, for the first six months, we became 'Internally Displaced Persons' inside the Kurdish territory of Syria. Then we escaped to Iraq and stayed there as refugees in camps for three and a half years. There I started to work with *Médecins sans Frontières*. I was a medical translator for them for six months, and a logistics officer for a year and a half. I also worked with the international humanitarian medical organisation *Première Urgence Internationale* for a year and a half. But to escape from ISIS in Iraq, we then had to flee to Turkey. And we stayed there for four months.

It was very difficult and expensive to live in Turkey because the government wasn't giving any help to refugees there. So I decided to try to use the rest of my savings to get us to Germany, mainly because the rest of my family had gone there. Unfortunately, I was cheated by human smugglers several times while trying to do this, and ended up having used up all my savings - more than 30,000 euros! Two months ago, I made it to the Idomeni Refugee Camp in Greece with my wife and baby, who had been born in the refugee camp in Iraq.

Unfortunately our baby got sick in the Idomeni Refugee Camp here in Greece. The conditions were much worse than they had been at the Domiz Camp in Iraq. The situation was really awful, although washing facilities at least were okay and people had access to toilets and showers. They had electric buckets there - they managed to use them to heat milk. However most of the time the refugees had to pay for any food they could get, and for any warm water. But health care was good. *Médecins Sans Frontières*, *Médecins du Monde* and the International Committee of the Red Cross did a good job of managing to treat the refugees, together with some volunteer doctors.

But the good news about the Idomeni Refugee Camp is that it's over! The Greek authorities moved the refugees away to other camps in Thessaloniki - more than 30 camps that have better provision and are better organised, with washing facilities. With my wife and child I live in a tent in these camps now, and work as a volunteer involved in translation, logistics and teaching.

On a typical day I wake up and take a shower with cold water. If it's raining or windy, I turn around our tent and fix it with iron bars. With my wife and baby to feed, after getting washed I go to the food distribution line and if it's proper food, I take it. If it's not, I try to buy food instead, by collecting wood that people can use for cooking. If we need milk for the baby I have to buy it.

Then I do volunteer work till night. For me life is a bit different than it is for most refugees because I speak four languages - Kurdish, Arabic, English and a bit of Iranian. So I spend all my time translating and interpreting, especially doing medical interpreting work. And I'm always asking the UN refugee agency questions, but they always reply that they don't know!

There are many diseases from life in the camp: diarrhoea, vomiting, abdominal pain, coughing, infections, runny noses and fever. There are also various disabling chronic diseases, and many other illnesses too. But I am always worried too about the fighting that takes place in the camps because of the many nationalities, religions and different points of view that have to live all together in the tents here. The Macedonian police sometimes let off tear gas, making both kids and adults struggle for breath.

I often feel the future is actually quite dark for Syrian refugees. But I try to have hope and focus on the humanitarian work I'll be able to do in the future together with other teachers and good people. We can organise and do a great job of providing all the children in the refugee camps with an education. I was always thinking already about helping people in need but the idea of helping kids was new to me.

I had the idea after I saw that children at the Domiz Camp where I was staying in Iraq were learning a language which is completely different from that taught by governmental schools! They weren't learning to write in Iranian or Arabic, nor to speak Kurdish. I thought that those kids were wasting their time without an education, and they were going to miss opportunities for their future. So I decided to set up a school where they could also learn the English language as well, which could help them build their future. So I guess I'm the founding 'heart' of the *Heart School* that we set up for refugee children in the Domiz Camp in Iraq.

Eventually I plan to settle down wherever I can to do humanitarian work, because that has always been my life-long plan. But what is urgently needed here at the moment is medical care and supplies because this is just a transit camp. And we also need support for the volunteers who are teaching the kids: the kids are the real victims of this war. I feel that one of the best ways to help the refugees at the moment is to support their children's education. '*By education, we can change a nation!*', I always say.

What I wish most for the future of my own family? My greatest wish is to be able to give my child a good education so that when he grows up, he can be sure that he will be able to take care of himself, and I need not worry about having to help him as an adult…

But here's some good news: my family is now within the process of the European Union Resettlement Programme. Two months ago we had the interview, and we are now waiting for a call from the embassy to hear whether they have decided that we will be allowed to move out of this Greek refugee camp into the EU, and apply for asylum somewhere in the EU.

By the way, you told me that you are Irish. You asked if I've ever met any Irish people or had friends from Ireland. Well yes, I have! I had an Irish friend, Karen - she was our Field Coordinator at one of the camps. The EU Resettlement organisation asked us to choose eight countries we might be sent to. Of course it would be great if we got asylum in Cambridge but I've chosen Ireland as one of the countries. If we could go to Ireland, it would be the dream of all dreams. I want to be there more than anywhere. I'm so happy to have your friendship here online - that is unforgettable. But for sure, I would love to meet your family in Ireland too, and visit with them. So *hopefully*...!

Unfortunately no one called me yet since our interview. I don't know if it's going to work. We are suffering and running out of our last money, with many needs and difficulties and expenses, but we always have hope...

[He logs off.] Sorry, I have to go. I'll talk to you again in an hour. I have to help out at the food-distribution line.

[Later...] Hello. So sorry I had to cut off earlier. It was a very busy day. I was working as a volunteer helping the medical team by translating between them and their patients, and then helping to distribute various aid.

I don't get to see any TV news but I see news here on Facebook. And I was really upset to see the attacks by some Middle Eastern men in Germany this week. I don't know what's going to happen to our application for resettlement now... Europeans are great people. I love them. But I always worry about my own relatives in Germany too....

Anyway, yesterday I was in the two other refugee camps here in Thessaloniki. And I want to tell you about some of the people I met there.

I've typed out on my mobile phone three long pieces that I'm going to try to send to you bit by bit over the next few days…

Alexandreia Refugee Camp, Thessaloniki

In Alexandreia Camp there are about 700 people - Kurdish Syrians and Arabic Syrians - living together. It's one of the worst camps in Greece. Shiar was one of a group of six people I met there yesterday who are converts from Islam to Christianity. As this is a humanitarian situation we have to remember not to make any kind of discrimination, or ignore anyone. And those guys are so happy to have converted! Shiar was telling me that more people would like to convert but it's difficult because of the big difference between our traditions, and the fear that other members of one's family - brothers, moms, fathers - could be punished by the extremists. He pointed out too that he will not able to go back to Syria because everyone knows he would be killed by the extremists for changing his religion. He explained that in their eyes, 'to follow Jesus is a crime'. But he said 'I am sure that one day, everyone will realise that Jesus is the right way to God.'

For me it's all just about the humanitarian work, but it was interesting to sit down for a while with those guys and to hear about their situation and experiences. They said these are the worst days they've ever had. Very bad food, very poor washing facilities, running out of money, not able to buy a few cigarettes or other personal things...

Shiar asked me if I could help him financially. He said he hasn't had anything proper to eat since two weeks ago when they were moved here from the Idomeni Camp - the worst camp on earth. He said: 'I had thought there could be nothing worse than Idomeni but I was shocked that the new camps are much worse! Five months ago I left Syria because they wanted me to join the military service - and I don't want to be a killer. But saying no to them means death. So you only have two options: join the fight or escape from Syria.'

I asked him 'Where are you now concerning the EU Relocation Programme?' He said 'I just don't know - my way is very dark. At the beginning they told us it will take only two months to hear back. But it's been about three months that I've been waiting now. Just a few days ago I got registered - or 'pre-registered' - but there is a rumour that we are going to have to wait in this awful camp for another year, or two years more!

And I am getting sick just thinking about it all the time. I've started to have bad dreams. I feel out of breath at midnight so I wake up in the night and spend a lot of time just smoking. I'm starting to have mental problems. I'm going crazy...'

I asked him whether, if the war ended, he would go back to Syria? He said 'Sure! I'd prefer one day in the oldest city in the world (*he meant Damascus*) than one year in Europe - there's no comparison!' Finally he wanted to thank the Greek people for their hospitality. He said 'We all know the financial crisis the Greek people are having themselves...'

On my way back to our own camp, I decided to stop off and visit the Darvini Camp, which contains 1,500 Syrian refugees who had to flee from their homes and come asking for asylum in Greece.

Darvini Refugee Camp, Thessaloniki

Most of the refugees in this camp are very well-educated Kurdish Arabs. But they are living in very bad conditions in the camp, really suffering from the awful infrastructure. There is no decent food. The army give out military food but it is really bad, with no nourishment. And there are no decent hygiene facilities - like toilets, showers or washing points.

They need food, they need clothes and many, many other things. Like milk for the kids, special items for pregnant women, toys for the kids… There's no medical treatment. There's no schooling provided for the children. One of these refugees, Dalila, told me her little boy had been sick for several days but she couldn't get access to a hospital. She said he was sick from the bad food.

Razan, a refugee from Aleppo, said to me: 'Even in our own country in the middle of the war, we did not suffer like we are suffering here... Here we are dying slowly. Dying slowly...'

Those people in the Darvini Camp are really in need. They are really pleading for help. They have no idea when the war in Syria will end. But meanwhile, I feel that we refugees must behave in a really good way - because we are representing our country here, and our religion. And we can communicate that to everyone by showing good behaviour. We have to try to behave as normally as we behaved before the war ever started...

It was there, in the Darvini Camp, that I met Juhan, a woman from Kurdish Syria, the mother of three little girls. She is on her own with them, along with her young brother. Her husband had to flee from Syria three years ago because he refused to join the army. And his family were left behind. He succeeded in getting asylum in Germany in 2013. But due to a problem with his application, he couldn't apply to bring his family officially to join him there. So he decided to try to bring them illegally via the Balkan way, as that was still open at that time.

Juhan talked to me about their life in Syria before the war. 'It was *peace of mind, peace of life...*' she said. 'My husband was working well as a taxi driver. Our kids were going to school. We had a very beautiful house. We'd visit with family, relatives, friends... We didn't even have to think about things like food or shelter. Or fear... On every day off, we'd go on a picnic. And I'll never forget that everyday moment of preparing the lunch and waiting for my kids and husband to come back home to eat together at midday...'

I asked her: 'What was the best thing about life back home, that you miss the most?' She started crying and said: 'When my husband would come back home, his hands full of good things and gifts of food. And I will never forget either my morning coffee that I used to have in our garden, in the early mornings...'

'How has life changed for you now?', I asked her. She said 'Life for me now is like as if you had bought some very nice clothes and someone took them from your hands and laid them down into the very dirty mud. That's how life is for us now.'

I asked her how it all started, how these changes came. She explained: 'Back home, we started to see very young guys carrying weapons, and then there was military action everywhere. We started to hear protests against the Syrian regime. After that many groups were founded to fight against each other. The news was all of kidnappings, killings... The action of death was everywhere. Then both the regime groups and the Kurdish fighters started forcing all men to join up and fight. My husband and I discussed the issue and we decided that he must leave the country...'

Why did you not go with him? I asked.

'We couldn't afford for us all to go. At that time the Balkan way was not yet open, so it was very expensive.'

How did you leave later, with your kids and young brother?, I asked her.

'My husband, speaking to me on the phone from Germany - he motivated me. He said 'Come, the Balkan way is open now. The trip will be not as expensive as it was before'. He said 'Sell everything now, including the house."

Can you talk about the journey from Syria to Turkey to here in Greece, and how it was for you?, I asked.

'I sold everything we had to be able to afford the journey. My husband had worked 15 hours a day in Syria trying to make sure that our kids would have a good future. I sold everything until we had enough money to leave. It was very, very difficult to go from Kurdish Syria across the border into Turkey. It was very scary. The border guards were opening fire on people at times, and we were hearing that news just before leaving! Finally we decided to go, with my three children and young brother. Four times we tried to cross the border into Turkey before succeeding. We payed 1,500 euros to get across - 300 euros for each of us.

After we'd been in Turkey for two weeks the smuggler called, to move us by boat to Greece. The smuggler put 152 of us on a boat. When we saw that boat, many of us wanted to go back, because his promise had been that there would only be 70 people on the boat. But then he told us that anyone who turned back would not get any refund. So we had no choice…

Both the lower compartment and the deck were totally filled with people. Waves began to come into the boat. The captain told everyone to throw their baggage into the sea. Then, in the ocean, we hit a rock. The captain told us not to worry. Water began to come into the boat, but again he told us not to worry. We were in the lower compartment and it began to fill up with water. It was packed too tight to move. Everyone began to scream. We were the last ones to get out of there alive. My brother pulled me out through the window, and he pulled out my kids.

In the ocean, he took off his life jacket and gave it to a woman. We all swam for as long as possible. After several hours he told me that he was too tired to swim anymore and that he was just going to float on his back and rest for a while. It was so dark we couldn't see anything. The waves were high. I could hear him calling to me but he just got further and further away…

Eventually a boat found me and my little girls, and later they found my brother too. But unfortunately a lot of people who were with us on that boat did not survive. Like one family that we had been friends with all the time that we were in Turkey - they drowned…'

How is life here in Greece for you as refugees?

'Being here is still better than to have stayed in Syria because staying there would have meant death. Here it's safe, but it's not good. The food, the shelters, the hygiene are all bad. We are suffering from such poor infrastructure. There is no schooling for our kids. We are not allowed to work. There are no answers to our questions, and the future looks very dark for us…'

[Kanwar logged off for an hour, then reappeared, typing...] Sorry, Marella. My phone broke there for a while but I've managed to fix it again. Here's the rest of my interview with Juhan...

I asked Juhan: How do you think the European people can help?

'The people in Greece are very welcoming - they are really good people. But Europeans could help more by offering more nourishing food, and medical facilities and treatments. Even just by standing beside us, smiling and laughing with our kids. They could support our kids by sending toys... For instance, Europe's support has meant that these precious little souls, my kids, got to eat *bananas* on the streets of Thessaloniki!! Fresh fruit! And your support can mean cleaner, warmer clothes, better facilities to have a personal wash... Your donations make the difference between people having a dinner in the evening, or going to sleep hungry. Or eating tasteless, bland, repetitive military food that's not nourishing or say, having a nutritious piece of fresh fruit - something we used to take for granted! I cannot even begin to tell you how much all these people need support...'

Do you feel that European people care about you?

'Yes, sure - we love them and they love us. They are very good people. But then there are some bad Middle Eastern people who come between us too - acting bad. Then some other bad people in Europe react against them, and they turn that same behaviour against all of us. I mean, concerning migration policy, if my country recovered and peace spread in our city again - for sure I would go right back! People in Europe need to understand that we *want* to go home - but we cannot at the moment because there's war there.

So I am in Greece now. I've tried eight times now to go illegally to Germany with the children to join my husband, but each time they brought us back by force. They say we have to apply through the European Union Relocation Programme, and it takes a long time. I have had my first interview for it, but we must wait over six months for the next interview. It's causing us so many ongoing difficulties and expenses...'

[Kanwar interjects…] Marella, my wife is sick, I must log off to look after her. You told me to tell her you look forward to having tea with her in her apartment in a nice European city one day in the future. She liked that. You have a nice mind. One of my skills is not to forget people who ever help me in any way. You are helping us right now, so you are one of those who are unforgettable during our suffering. Thank you.

[Two days later…] Hi, I'm back online now. I just want to tell you about one person I won't ever forget, whatever happens - a little boy called Rami. He came up to me and said 'Please, sir, can you help my mom? She's hungry…' He was trying to get some food from me for her, but I didn't have any at that time. So I said to him 'Can you take me to her? I want to see what she needs…' He took me to where his mom was. She explained: 'I lost my husband in the war in Syria. There's only me now to take care of our two little girls and our little boy here in the camp.'

I asked her gently: 'Do you need something? Are you sick because of hunger?' She cried '*No!*' So I said 'Oh, I'm sorry - it was just that your little boy said to me…' And she cried out 'Oh, my God…!' and started weeping. She said: 'It's true that two days ago, we didn't have any food at all. My kids went to bed that night without eating anything. So now he is scared of having to go through another night like that ever again. That is why he went and spoke to you…'

That was something unbelievable - somehow it really broke my heart, that moment. Something made me silent and I couldn't even speak. I just turned away. As you know, I am a refugee myself in the same situation, with my own wife and baby to feed. But I could not leave them there without giving them something. So I gave them the last 20 euros that I had left. That was all that I had - all I could give them.

You know, to live just for oneself must be a terrible existence. I always think: *'Give your life for something much larger than yourself. Live for a greater reality. Leave a legacy…'*

I had nothing else to give her but I could also give her my name. I said to her: 'My name is Kanwar Ali: please call me if you have such a night again.'

I can't offer you any kind of closure, reader, on this, the book's final interview. Kanwar - by choosing to walk his own interview out into the camps and extend it to the other refugees around him - has opened this chapter out onto the near-infinity of other refugee voices that urgently need to be heard... He has brought us to the side of a hungry child. A single mother. A group of 'apostates' - converts from Islam to Christianity. A man who thinks he's losing his mind... There are 50,000 others in those Greek camps, 67,000 more in the Domiz Camp that Kanwar came from in the Iraqi desert, and millions piled into Turkey and Lebanon.

The speakers in this book's other chapters told of the futures they embraced after receiving asylum. But for Kanwar and these others, there is no future *visible* right now, not to mind embraceable. They speak with focused, burning hope of the interviews they've had for the EU Resettlement Programme. But my heart sinks: that's the stingy process for implementing our countries' infamous *'refugee quotas'*.

But even in this situation - where there is nothing - Kanwar is all about *creating* something. He creates in the void so that there will be something to share and to give, which seems to be the whole point of life, as far as he's concerned. While penniless, sleeping on the ground for years on end in destitute camps among the abandoned thousands, he has created for himself a full-time job delivering all day every day a full portfolio of skills and services. In these camps, he hasn't had a day off 'work' in years... He just ignores the fact that he isn't paid anything for any of it.

And while drifting - desperate and displaced - from camp to camp, he also built from scratch a romance, a marriage and a little family... On Valentine's Day in 2014 in the Iraqi camp, he married the beautiful, radiantly smiling Khaleji - a woman in love. And sturdy baby Daniel, with the piercing, intelligent, brown eyes, was born there a year and a half later. (That's Kanwar holding Daniel in the photo at the start of this chapter on page 188.)

And then Kanwar reached out spontaneously to me across the internet on that hot night while I sat lounging in my glass extension in Cambridge. He popped onto my laptop screen to say hallo, and from that greeting he went on to create out of nothing an online friendship with me, then this book chapter, and now his encounter here with you, his reader...

So with him, it's never about closure. Despite sitting in the dust with nothing but a faulty old mobile phone, he's all about creating new beginnings. New encounters, new lives to hear about and share, new lesson-plans to think up for the kids' classes in the mud tomorrow...

Through the miracles of internet technology, Kanwar is 'in' Cambridge with me now like the book's other interviewees are. Because wherever our bodies are physically sitting - whether in the mud or in high-tech Cambridge or wherever you are reading these pages - we are all in this together now in these virtual spaces where we can communicate, chat, befriend, learn, publicise, campaign, vote, lobby, send donations, send consolations...

So there's no need to just close this book now, reader. Instead, you can come on in, explore and make some new friends of your own. For instance, you can take a surprisingly enjoyable online stroll around the Domiz Refugee Camp in Iraq, and see its positive, uplifting aspects for yourself. At http://refugeerepublic.submarinechannel.com there is an interactive feast of sounds, videos, drawings and interviews where the camp's refugees invite you into their little tent-homes to see all the day to day things they are doing there. You will really feel as if you've been there on an intriguing visit that has charm, courtesy and humour...

Meanwhile https://techfugees.com is a worldwide network of internet technology experts who are boosting this interconnectedness of refugees in other ingenious ways. The charismatic Syrian refugee Hassan Akkad - the war-torn star of the BBC *Exodus* films pictured on the opening page of this book - told me he was in Cambridge the other day and 'loved the city', giving a talk at *Techfugees Cambridge* about the resourceful ways that technology can help us all to help refugees worldwide.

At www.youtube.com/watch?v=DsKspazsbTI, you can have a look at Kanwar's intimate slideshow of the people he has just interviewed for us in his chapter above. And at www.livingrefugeearchive.org, you will be able to follow his ongoing story as it will unfold over the time ahead, after the publication of this book. As I write the last pages of this book, nobody knows what will happen to him and Khaleji and the baby. At the University of East London's online Living Refugee Archive, you can read the news and further interviews he hopes to send on about what's happening to them in the Greek camps, in the EU Relocation Programme and beyond. As the outcomes for him and his family are as yet unknown, the Living Refugee Archive is the best place for you to discover how they will unfold in the future…

# Understanding…

It's been many years now since the opening scene of this book when I looked out onto a sea of studious faces, giving my first lecture after arriving from France to work at Cambridge University. Against all my expectations, I stayed in this strange city a long time, initially for work. Then I married the English-born medical scientist son of Stefan, the Polish interviewee in chapter nine. So Stefan became my father-in-law, and the international wedding that he described in his chapter was mine.

But in the six months since the last of this book's interviews, the world has changed radically around us all (a bit like the way it changed around each interviewee in their home country before they fled). Suddenly the roles, rights, identities and freedoms of hundreds of millions of us are being shuffled again in the most unprecedented shake-up of nationalities since Stefan was brought here as a war-refugee in 1946. After the recent 'Brexit' referendum, this country is now to spend the next few years leaving the European Union in favour of a right-wing, free-market alliance with Donald Trump, who was sworn in as US President the other day. Yesterday he announced a blanket ban against any citizens of seven Middle Eastern countries even entering the US: those in transit are being detained and deported as I write.

So in our own personal reshuffle, my husband and I are applying to live on the continent before Brexit is completed, because we don't want to be part of Britain's new direction. As an Irish and hence European citizen, I am grateful that I will have the ongoing right to live freely in Europe. But my husband, though an eminent scientist, won't have those rights any more after Brexit, because he's an English citizen. So he has engaged a solicitor to apply for Polish citizenship for him, based on his father's nationality. Like so many of my interviewees, we now find ourselves awaiting the outcome of a citizenship hearing, this time in a Warsaw court. If it is successful, we will travel to Poland to present our thanks, along with copies of this book to deposit in the Town Hall and public library in Bydgoszcz, where Stefan grew up and was taken captive by the Nazis as a teenager. These twists in all our national futures were unimaginable even a year ago. Now no-one knows what the further future will hold for our societies.

As on my first morning in Cambridge in front of the sea of student faces, my notes are in front of me again now this morning, and I am about to speak again. I'm in a different building this time, but it's just across the road from my old College at the University. This too is a very formal environment, full of role and ritual. Each seat at this long table has its own microphone, anchored with buttons that light up. Wooden place-names with important job titles mark out the hierarchy of places to sit. As in the College, here too there is a great deal of ceremony around *The Chair*, the figure who thrones at the top of the table, surrounded by whispering advisors.

This great table, almost entirely filling the long chamber, reminds me of *High Table* at the College but also of that English legend, the *Knights of the Round Table*. As far as I can see, tables seem to be an important symbol in English culture. In the other cultures that I know well, tables are just for laying the food on: collective ritual there is *all about the food*. But here tables seem to have a different function, namely to apportion rank - that mainstay of English culture, its organising principle. Here tables are not for feeding an amorphous human mass, but for structuring them into an ordered, governed hierarchy.

Around this table today are ranked the elected politicians who govern this famous city. This is their parliament and voting-chamber, a regional micrcosm of the national one. A few have upper-class accents but as many are working-class. Unemployed working-class people with disabilities have been elected here, and Black working-class residents. One of the Black African women involved in this book's outreach programme has now been elected to the chamber and is sitting further down the table. I'm here today as a paid advisor to the politicians, to report on strategies and policies for engaging the city's poor (who are predominantly the White English underclass), and getting them participating in democracy. The purpose of that work is to get excluded voices heard and organising, and eventually elected into this governing chamber.

As I await my turn to speak, it occurs to me that the formal, hierarchical rituals of Cambridge culture still feel as foreign to me as they first did twenty years ago. But in the meantime I've learned that *nationality* per se is even less meaningful than we used to think it was. I've learned that in reality, it's the sharing of values, legislation, working life and culture that holds a given population together in a weave of solidarity that is more important than the nationality of individuals. Isn't it the case that all over the world, groups like refugees, small farmers, student-protesters, unemployed labourers or oppressed women have more in common with each other than with the elites of their own nationality who are oppressing them?

From listening to the speakers in this book, it seems to me now that the reason refugees are flooding to Europe is not just for its wealth or for its work but primarily to live under the protections of its *civil society*, in the fullest political sense of the term. For a population to self-organise into a civil society, it needs four supporting pillars: legislation protecting human rights and freedom of speech; an independent judiciary and police to enforce it; free democratic elections for accountable leadership and policies; and a free press to keep the whole system transparent and challenged. An advanced, prosperous civil society adds three further layers to these, namely robust taxation that redistributes excessive wealth; quality free education, healthcare and other public services funded from those taxes; and a welfare net supporting the vulnerable and paying a state pension to the elderly.

It seems to me that these are the structures that refugees and other migrants most envy us for, and the biggest reason for their wanting to join our society. It's not just for the infamous capitalist wealth in our countries: after all, they see a lot of ostentatious wealth in their own countries too - it's just that it tends to be corruptly hoarded by a tiny, militarised elite. Yes, the European Union is over three times wealthier than the average for countries worldwide - but it spends *over seven times the world average* on providing public services for its citizens. [23]

The crucial thing about this civil society mechanism - whether in the west or in the devleoping world - is that if any element in the supporting chain is missing, the whole structure collapses into abuses that no longer safeguard the majority and the vulnerable. For instance, in much of the developing world, there is lots of private wealth - there's just no attempt to redistribute it through taxes and public services. There's usually an extremely strong judiciary and police force - it's just that they're often there to brutalise the population and ring-fence protection around the elites. There's often an excellent education available to the children of that elite - it's just not made available to everyone else. And there are often elections for political office - but no free media informing an educated population to ensure those elections are democratic and transparent. [24]

But these chain-links that hold civil society together can only be built and sustained by all of us - the whole population ourselves. Like an ant-hill or a bee-hive, it requires the full collective participation of all the individuals in it to get the job done. The population must demand free elections and progressive policies, stand for office themselves, go out and vote in the elections, demand and engage with independent media that critique the system, use the public services of free education and healthcare... Many must study, train and qualify to earn their living delivering those services. All must spend a large chunk of their life-time earning a living, paying substantial taxes and obeying the rule of law... Right down to not dropping litter in the street, it is we ourselves, the people, who rebuild every day this hive of structures that protect our collective quality of life. Without the billions of contributions that we ordinary individuals make to it every single week, the structure would dissolve by the following week.

In my own long journey as a visitor trying to get to know who this country really is, I feel that all the 'digging' I've done for this book's interviews has finally revealed to me what England really is, and who its

[23] Nougayrède, N., 2017. 'Europe in crisis? Despite everything, its citizens have never had it so good' in *The Guardian*, 1-4-2017
[24] I traced the task of building this civil society 'chain' in developing countries in my chapter 'Corruption and human rights - The potentials' in the international book *Human Rights and Good Governance - Building Bridges* (ed. Sano & Alfredsson), Danish Institute of Human Rights & Martinus Press, 2000.

heroes really are. From the day I arrived, I had never believed in '*Brand Britain*' - the PR image that associates Englishness with elites. Top-hatted toffs, pin-striped bankers, Oxbridge dons, horsey aristocrats, TV celebrities, Etonians, media-makers, pop stars, luxury-brand consumers… Having sat so long with the refugees and having worked for a local authority, I've seen under the skin of England now. England: I can look you square in the eyes now because I know who you really are.

I know your hidden bones - who the real heroes are here, under the disguising cloak of glamour. I've seen that England's real heroes are the millions of ordinary, good-hearted working and volunteering people who tenderly hold this society together through their daily labours for it. The nurses, carers, teachers, benefits officers, jobcentre staff. The housing officers, librarians, road sweepers, bin men, food-bank volunteers. The charity workers, ambulance drivers, football coaches, care-home workers, municipal gardeners, litter-pickers…

This is the vast, well-organised tissue of ordinary human goodness - the supporting fabric. Beneath the aristocratic pomp and the luxe consumerism of *Brand Britain* (ie. the media pretence that it's elites who make this country), this is what English society is, behind the scenes, actually very good at. If you fall unconscious in the street here without a penny in your pocket, if your life falls apart, these strangers will be there for you. As organised as a colony of bees, coordinated as ants on the march, an organised army of civil society and public workers will gather you up and look after you.

These things are the pinnacle of modernity, and something that western cultures must remain proud of. They debunk the myth that accumulated private wealth and capitalist competition are the west's biggest achievements. In reality, this dedicated, labour-intensive weave of services and support for everyone is actually the west's peak achievement: millions of ordinary working and volunteering people, looking after many millions of people and places. In my opinion, this is the modern miracle - the peak of economic development - and a way of using our prosperity that we don't need to feel ashamed of. It's easy to feel chronically guilty every time we switch on the television and see the countless millions across the planet who live without anything like these services and supports. But feeling guiltily over-privileged isn't an appropriate reaction. Everyone, including ourselves, deserves this support and deserves to see society's wealth reinvested for the collective good around them in this way. I believe that the best reaction is to actively defend and extend these collective services. Even in western countries, they could disappear for all of us overnight if we the public allowed politics to swing in a direction that favoured only private wealth and services.

Sitting here waiting to speak in this ancient voting chamber, I reflect with a sigh that the shortcomings of the democratic process are obvious. There's still plenty of room for improvement. But compared to being ruled over by multi-national shareholders or a military junta, a police state or religious militia, civil society democracy is the best option we've got at the moment and it's one we can build on. With a nod from one of the officials, the button on my microphone lights up and I lean in and speak.

Conclusion

If memory, conversation and listening have been the *medium* of this project, what have been its *messages*? For me, four themes stand out as common ground in these very diverse life stories, and all four of them surprised me. They were:

- how much the speakers longed to be listened to
- the centrality of hospitality traditions in their lives
- how intensely connected they remained, both mentally and materially, to their home countries and to compatriots who have migrated from there
- the profound ambivalence they felt towards English society, principally because they felt it would never let them 'in' - let them feel or become 'English' - even if they officially gained citizenship

Reviewing these four themes, it's interesting how interconnected they are, one almost flowing organically from the next. In terms of hospitality traditions, most seemed to feel in a visceral way that I didn't really know them - we weren't friends yet - until we had eaten and drunk something together, however simple, in their home or in a restaurant from their culture where they could be the host and invite me. (This was so for the Polish and Irish interviewees as much as for those from the Middle East and Africa.)

My most iconic, moving memory of these hospitality-ceremonies was the project's very first cup of tea, served to me by Ruth at the start of the first chapter. It was lukewarm and watery and had involved a lot of trips out from her bedsit out into the draughty corridor to prepare it. As we perched on the bed in her dark, cramped little room, Ruth served it to me with the joy and pride of a queen finally serving a queen.

Stefan's wine and olives. Fionn's homemade banana cake. Habibah's oven-fresh almond biscuits and cardamom-brewed coffee. Saoirse's high tea at the grand hotel. Adar's Turkish restaurant. I loved sharing these unexpected pleasures with the interviewees, because I too miss so much here in England the daily food rituals that bind you into the collective culture of other countries. (I had moved here from France, where food is *the* civic glue.) For these interviewees, hospitality and sharing food with neighbours seemed to be the life-altering, strategic connector that knits people together, proactively building solidarity even across deep divides of class, ideology, ethnicity and circumstance.

Here in England, ironically, their love of doing this sets them apart rather than binding them in. It jars because it feels so un-English. An Englishman's home is, after all, his castle - an intensely private space. In English culture, meals and eating are a private activity, done with intimates and closed groups, not a semi-public ceremony for carefully bonding with acquaintances outside the edges of one's social circle. [25]

While they recognised that English society was 'welcoming' at a cool, administrative level in granting asylum, almost all seemed to find it excluding at an emotional and civic level, compared to the sense of public companionship and national fellowship they were used to in their own culture. Most saw the great practical desirability of gaining British citizenship as a stamped document. But it seemed that none could envisage ever being allowed to *become* or *feel English* - being invited or expected to feel completely part of Englishness.

It seemed that the English gave them the impression that Englishness is something you can only be born into. (And, as we observed in the introduction, many of them knew that by contrast, identities like 'Frenchness' or 'being Scandinavian' are detailed codes of personal behaviour, lifestyle and civic values that an immigrant in those countries is actively *expected* to adopt and fully participate in.)

Perhaps this difficulty in forming closer bonds with the English is a small part of why all these interviewees, no matter how long they had been here, remained intensely connected to the home country and to compatriots

---

[25] Anthropologist Kate Fox explores this in the ethnography of English culture already cited in the Introduction, *Watching the English – The hidden rules of English behaviour*, Hodder & Stoughton, 2014

here, no matter how conflicted those relationships might be. I noticed that inner suffering over the home country's difficulties doesn't ever seem to go away for them. It seemed a painful cocktail of concern for loved ones, neighbours and colleagues still back home; feeling guilty for having better living conditions here themselves; and sending money and moral support back home as best they could, but feeling powerless to do any more.

These four themes - listening, hospitality, connectedness and a disappointment around belonging - lead on to the single thing that struck me most about all the speakers: namely, the range of creative, adaptive strategies that they improvise to navigate the passions, ambivalences and disappointments above.

Creative strategies

The interviews reveal the dense network of resourceful strategies that individual speakers improvise to circumvent their social, psychological and political challenges. But all the interviewees raised as well, unprompted, the subject of racism, mentioning eight different types of experiences they had in England that they considered racist.

First, there were historical memories of types of racism that are no longer legal, like the 'No dogs, no spitting, no Irish' signs in chapter eight. Second, there was shaming of a refugee child because of the poverty in which she arrived and the fact that they were 'Boat People'. Third, there were the present-day, physical manœuvres of White English women who wouldn't sit next to Ruth's Black African woman-friend on the bus and fourth, the fabricated tales told to the housing authorities about Habibah in chapter seven.

Fifth, there were the workplace interactions where White English colleagues of the same or less ability got the promotions. Sixth, the feeling of being tolerated from a distance, but with the proviso that you could never *belong* to, acquire or adopt Englishness. Seventh, there was interviewees' sense of being unwillingly silenced - expected to hold their tongue now they're in England - about injustices and political sufferings still ongoing back home. And eighth, the pragmatic, competitive form of racism that has been driven by recent austerity, stoked by the scramble for scarce, insecure jobs and reduced public services.

Interestingly, in the interviews the speakers put more energy into describing the strategies they have evolved to circumvent racism, rather than dwelling on the problem itself. In all, they described over twenty different adaptive strategies that they apply in four different domains - the psychological, professional, cultural and civic.

They describe six different psychological strategies:

- deliberately ignoring racism and systematically teaching their peers to 'un-see' it (Ruth)

- internal self-talk, reminding themselves that they have *nothing to be ashamed of* (Hanh)

- self-talk that builds inner pride in their own survival story of near-death migration (Hanh)

- trying empathically to imagine the inner reasoning of the racist (Adar)

- researching the socio-historical reasons why Englishness as a national identity may be particularly 'un-absorbent' so that one can never become English, but only 'live among the English' (Adar)

- theatrically 'playing up' to the racist stereotype to make it their own (Fionn)

- political activism that tries to get the host country's authorities and public to '*listen*' (Fatima)

In the professional sphere, the interviews described three different ways that work was used to heal or circumvent the wounds of racism. One was by working so hard that there's no time or energy left to worry about what White English neighbours think of you. Whole generations of the extended family in chapter two '*work too hard*', as Hanh puts it, at the family takeaway business, to help forget past traumas. Another theme was setting very high educational and professional goals for their children, using the English educational system to coach children steadily towards entering the professions here. The strategy of Adar, in the tenth chapter, was to use his multi-lingual gifts to qualify as a Chartered Interpreter, now earning his living mediating between the Home Office and the asylum-seekers they interview.

The third branch of strategies the speakers used to circumnavigate racism was cultural and artistic. One Chinese community group toured the city giving lavishly-costumed performances of their traditional Chinese Dragon Dance, to educate non-Chinese audiences through entertainment. Fionn in chapter eight, though an autodidact, founded a substantial arts festival that came to be well respected as part of the city's cultural scene, staging culture from his own country for an English audience. We already noted his determination, despite being confined to bus-conducting, to signal his culturedness and overwhelm racist stereotypes by whistling classical music, speaking French to tourists and carrying 'a *big tome*' under his arm while he worked.

The fourth category of creative response to racism was the interviewees' extensive volunteer activism in civil society, which we already surveyed in the introduction. The dozens of volunteer roles that they embrace served multiple purposes in their lives. First, these activities are a routine part of the networked support-systems that migrant groups and ethnic communities create for themselves as a survival mechanism here and in other host countries. Companionship, support, spiritual counsel, practical advice, free training, free services, loans, job offers, accommodation and money-saving tips are just some of the resources that the interviewees exchange and barter for free on these networks. Secondly, this volunteer activism gives an outlet for the irrepressible political, altruistic and civic energies of certain individuals whose very commitment to civic activism was often what caused them to be persecuted by home country regimes in the first place.

Thirdly, volunteering can pave the way for entry into difficult English labour markets, providing work experience, training, language skills and references that might otherwise be unattainable, as Samir explained in chapter four. Lastly, it seems that volunteering and civic altruism can restore some of the self-esteem and pride lost in transit from their old life. If the surrounding English society happens to notice or grant them 'points' for it, so much the better, though I had the impression that the host society rarely notices this aspect of refugees' lives here.

Navigating rifts between themselves

Interviewees' strategies for navigating ideological rifts within their own community were equally creative. The Polish refugee used hospitality, inviting neighbours to his home or out to restaurants for food-celebrations, and he used games, distracting his compatriots from political disagreements by focusing on their national love of chess. The Irish in the city circumvented their internal disagreements on colonial and sexual politics by coming together around culture. They formed clubs giving lessons in Irish dance, singing, language and story-telling, where compatriots politely park their political differences. The Turkish community - riven with serious political differences around the Kurdish issue - put those aside when attending their regular 'Business Breakfasts'. Here everyone mingled around their national tradition of hospitality: the food was an ice-breaker enabling them to exchange practical help and advice for job-seeking, housing, parenting support and mental health.

The interviewees who practised religion tried to attend church, mosque or temple without discussing the home-country politics that often divided them. Part of the outreach project for this book involved a cultural exhibition led by African women, sharing foods and artefacts in an attempt to cut across deep internal divisions of both class and ideology. One of them, though an unemployed job-seeker, rose to elected public office through the municipal programme of empowerment that we ran, as described in the appendix. She also set up her own travel company to project a more positive image of her home country.

Refugees' political activism

Back in the introduction, we wondered what we would discover about interviewees' levels of political activity here in England. Do they mobilise politically? Their answers revealed a tangle of desires and constraints around mobilising. In fact, they named thirteen such factors - four affecting how they respond to class politics, three shaping their responses to sexual politics, and seven shaping their positions on immigration politics.

Their responses to class politics are shaped by a delicate balance of several issues, namely: their class background back home; their current class status here in England (which may have gone up or down, each direction potentially provoking a different political response); and the level of difference between their own current class status and that of their compatriots here. And their attitudes to class politics seem shaped most of all by their own class-aspirations here in England. Some, though by no means all, aspired to climb the English class-ladder.

In terms of sexual politics, the interviewees described experiences across the full spectrum - from Sharia law to complete sexual freedom. There were already private divergences between compatriots back home about sexual politics and freedoms, whatever official restrictions were imposed by the regime they lived under. And further divergences inevitably emerge amidst the new sexual freedoms potentially available here.

On immigration politics, the speakers hold no less than six different positions, namely:

- the integrationist attitude of keeping as low a profile as possible, 'keeping your head down' and not passing comment either publicly or privately on the subject

- the contrasting position of openly celebrating their ethnic pride and difference

- the option of trying to campaign publicly and raise awareness here about ongoing injustices in the home country

- not commenting any further on politics, often through sheer exhaustion, trauma and resignation at having had their own life ruined by their political activism in the home country in the first place

- feeling they are expected to 'stay quiet' about political issues once given asylum, silence being almost the 'price to pay' for permission to stay and get on with life here

- the more self-serving 'close the door behind me' attitude to immigration policy (as often exemplified by ethnic minority politicians in the Conservative and UKIP parties)

Given the tangle of variables above, it is perhaps no surprise that, despite many coming from very politicised backgrounds, the speakers showed little interest in getting involved in English party politics. Eight further variables coloured this. Any interest there was in Conservative politics seemed to come from interviewees who saw themselves as 'self-made' - self-employed business-people who felt they had received little support from their English neighbours in starting up, and so don't feel inclined towards any leftist solidarity with the nation's working classes now. Another group are those driven by upward class-aspirations here: they are not mobilising for class-equality or for the working classes either.

On the left, there are the many refugees here who opposed tyrannical regimes back home, but I found these to be disillusioned with governments per se. Disgusted, and often damaged, by their home government, they seem further disillusioned by what they see as the British government's inaction against that regime, or what they see as the 'wrong' action against it. Furthermore, they tend to see all mainstream British parties as having essentially the same foreign policies that they disagree with, whether on Palestine, the 'war on terror', immigration or human rights abuses.

These people - originally active and politicised back home - are unlikely to have the will or energy here to campaign on more universal issues of progressive politics such as trade unionism, feminism or the anti-austerity movement. They will campaign on injustices in their home country if on anything, but the interviews suggest they are more likely to pour those energies into local volunteer supports for their compatriots here, and for the wider civil society.

Outcomes for communities

This research project was designed to produce not just this book but also a range of specific outcomes for communities. The first level of outcome and learning in any oral history project is the personal experience of the encounter between the speaker and listener, and what they each take away from that.

With its empathic attentiveness, the oral history interview is initially a moment of private performance and encounter happening between two people. It's a privileged, heightened, relatively unpredictable communication outside of ordinary time on a subject that's important to both of them, though in different ways - personally and intimately to one, more theoretically and professionally to the other.

A second outcome of the project is the recording or transcript of that interview. It is necessarily a partial picture, as it doesn't record the atmospheres, inner emotions or unspoken thoughts that accompany the conversation on each side.

A book wrapped around or derived from those transcripts, like this book, is a third outcome that can allow some of those unspoken perceptions and reflections to be added back in, as I have done here in my brief commentaries before and after each interview.

As explained in the introduction, this book will also enjoy a fourth outcome, finding a permanent home as part of the Living Refugee Archive at the University of East London. The Living Refugee Archive celebrates the tool that is oral history, using it with refugee communities to build results-oriented partnerships between academia, the archive and community projects on the ground.

In that spirit, a fifth layer of outcomes from this project was the programme of community events and trainings that flowed from the learning gleaned from the interviews. That programme, as detailed in this book's appendix, translated the learnings into policy actions that are quite different from books or transcripts, so as to engage residents who might never read a book like this one.

Reading this book will have taken you personally on many journeys: first, down the side-streets into homes in the poorer parts of town and from there, out into the remembered worldwide journeys that brought this book's involuntary travellers to Cambridge. (Of the book's twelve travellers, I am the only one who came here voluntarily.) From their living-rooms, we travelled on into the labyrinth of social and political dilemmas that they must navigate in order to establish meaningful, productive lives here.

This project's purpose was not only to listen to, record or publish their stories but also to derive from them a set of policy outcomes that would be implemented by local authorities to help improve the lives and outcomes of refugees in England. So let's travel on further now and see what journeys were taken using the learning from the interviews, to ensure that those learnings moved beyond the oral history archive, to benefit communities through practical policy actions.

Implementing policy actions

After I had analysed the interviewees' core messages and recommendations, I was employed by local government to deliver a programme of diversity events and anti-racist trainings that took those learnings out into the host community, working face to face with hundreds of the surrounding White English residents in person, and with thousands through magazine publications.

Two important principles drove this outreach work. Firstly, it avoided preaching to the converted and instead took on the challenge of taking those messages to the hardest, most 'politically incorrect' audiences where those insights are needed most. Secondly, it was designed to ensure that all the learning involved in this project became *generative* learning, reproducing and disseminating itself at minimal cost, generating new levels of awareness in recipients, and enabling them in turn to take new steps that they might not have taken before. For anyone interested in delivering this kind of outreach programme, it's worth embracing those two priorities - tackling the most challenging audiences, and ensuring there's generative learning - as they add crucial, targeted value in this climate of public-funding cuts.

The trainings and events were delivered to the White English social housing tenants who form the local host community that physically surrounds our interviewees. Most of the interviewees live dispersed around the city's social housing estates. And almost 90% of social housing tenants in the city are White English. (Cambridge doesn't tend to have separate residential areas where specific ethnic minorities live. Its ethnic networks are dispersed across town.)

In my experience, White English social housing tenants are one of the toughest audiences in the country to deliver anti-racist training to. They are the poorest demographic in the country now, since English social housing is now allocated based on rigorously means-tested poverty and vulnerability. Even in affluent Cambridge, two-thirds of social housing tenants receive welfare benefits and two-thirds of that group who are of working age are classified as chronically too ill to work.[26]

Poverty and scarcity, especially in a climate of austerity and extreme welfare cuts, tend to breed racism. Obviously this is not just an English phenomenon: the racisms of different countries each have different flavours, fed by the nation's history, culture, collective psychology and media messages. But having worked at length with the poverty and alienation of the White English unemployed underclass, it seems to me that their post-Empire history, their socio-political context as a de-industrialised class within a multicultural workforce, and their vulnerability to radicalisation by right-wing tabloids can make a potent cocktail.

---

[26] By contrast, in Germany, Scandinavia or parts of the US, for instance, social housing can also be a middle-class phenomenon, often housing a liberal, educated, professional class.

There is currently no left-wing political party reaching out successfully to build solidarities for this community, and the trade union culture that used to nourish them is hugely weakened. As our interviewees lived dotted around this community, and I already had long experience of doing outreach work with this White English underclass, they were the obvious target audience for any learnings gleaned from the refugees' interviews. So the speakers' most useful insights were turned into a range of trainings and community outreach projects that I later delivered for local authorities.

The other driver cited above was that none of the learning be wasted, but rather that it be *generative*, provoking new learning and activism in those who encountered the project. We wanted to wring the maximum value possible from the oral histories, translating them into other media and seeding their messages in individuals who would in turn do something positive with them, passing that benefit on to someone else. So we tried to use multi-media strategies as creative and diverse as the ones we'd seen the refugee speakers use to tackle their own challenges. The five levels of policy actions we took are explained in the appendix, in case other projects or communities would like to use or adapt any of those strategies. As you can see in the appendix, we used methods as diverse as theatre, film, dance, journalism, games, role-play, exhibitions, food, one to one coaching and work experience. I am happy to be contacted at any time for advice on doing similar interventions yourself.

This has been a book of a dozen voices - all foreign, including my own. So let the last word go to two White English natives of this country where we foreigners are grateful to have been able to live. As collaborators of mine over the years in work with politics and communities, English colleagues like these have taught me three important things that I didn't yet know when I first arrived at High Table and Evensong. This political education that I got from working with them later on was not something I had been able to pick up in my time working at the University. From these colleagues I learned first, that the biggest problem in this country is not ethnicity or migration but the brutal *economic* inequalities that the country's policies impose on its own native population. Among the 49 richest countries of the developed world, the UK is the third most unequal, nurturing some of the fiercest contrasts between its rich and poor. [27] Secondly, I learned that those who languish long term at the bottom of this bitter pile are not migrants or refugees but the country's own native White underclass. (Research shows that over time, migrants fare much better than them in education and in the job market.)

The third thing I learned in my years working with these English colleagues is that whether we are in a foreign place or in our place of origin, whether we feel alienated or at home there, what unites us anywhere is never our nationality, but shared values and collective participation in shaping a just society together, wherever we are.

---

[27] These stark facts are explained in detail in *The Spirit Level - Why greater equality makes societies stronger* by Kate Pickett and Richard Wilkinson, Bloomsbury, 2011, and in *Inequality and the 1%* by Prof Danny Dorling of Oxford University, Verso Press, 2014.

Afterword

Terry Sweeney and Diana Minns [28]

Marella Hoffman's book uncovers and illustrates in very human, engaging ways the high levels of inequality in Cambridge. Each year at the University's famous May Balls, tuxedoed students pay up to £250 each to wine, dine and dance all night while consuming vast quantities of champagne. But how much awareness does their education give them of the cooks, waiters, bar tenders and security staff who work so hard to make their evening a success, despite being paid very low wages? Whoever put that *Reality Checkpoint* arrow on the lamp post dividing the 'two sides' of this city was prescient indeed!

We first read this book in the tumultuous days after the UK's vote to leave the EU. In the light of that decision, it would be easy to forget that England has been a safe haven for refugees - seekers of asylum - during all of its history. We are a mongrel nation shaped by invasions and empire, immigration and emigration.

The life stories in this book confront and confound the stereotypes of asylum-seekers currently peddled in the media and by many others. Taking an approach that is gently probing, enabling, respectful and reflective, Marella Hoffman has revealed the reality of lives left behind, and the struggles to make a new life in a new country.

In our own work, we have always been impressed and humbled by the sheer guts and courage of those who often overcome terrible adversities,

---

[28] Terry Sweeney is a former Mayor of Cambridge, and was an elected politician with Cambridge City Council. Diana Minns is employed by Cambridge Women's Resources Centre. A former Councillor and Committee leader for a London Borough, she has worked with the homeless and is a resident representative with Cambridge City Council. The views expressed here are their own, not those of any organisations.

fighting to make a success of the rest of their lives. It is saddening to see some of our fellow citizens turn their backs on such brave people.

Normally, such 'everyday' lives are not well documented. Our history is based on big events and tales of the powerful and famous - kings and queens. The life of the migrant or asylum-seeker is usually outside our circle of concern and reality. That is why this book and the lives it shares are so important and significant for us all. Everyone has a tale to tell, and these pages give voice to those who would otherwise be unheard, ignored - or have their story misrepresented by others.

One of us, Terry, was born in Cambridge but it wasn't until he won a scholarship to the expensive Perse School that he began to see the two halves of the city. Until then, he had grown up quite happily in a working class area and knew little about the University or the wealthier parts. The Perse was an eye-opener. The school uniform and its dreaded cap identified you as a '*Perse pig*', drawing insults shouted by boys from the more 'ordinary' schools.[29]

The masters wore gowns and the prefects were empowered to beat you - to 'give you the slipper' - if you dared commit some minor misdemeanour. The boys too were different. There were a few other scholarship boys but most were paid for by wealthy parents (though the school did treat all its students the same). As well as the difference in economic backgrounds, the school included diverse ethnicities. Terry's class had boys from China, Indonesia and a boy from Africa who - it was rumoured - was the son of a powerful tribal chief. (He would neither confirm nor deny it!) Terry was lucky to have come across such diversity at such a young age, because most young people in Cambridge at that time wouldn't have encountered it until much later. As part of the programme of policy actions listed here in the appendix, Terry and Marella Hoffman together

---

[29] The school was founded 400 years ago as an offshoot of one of the Cambridge University Colleges. Its fees are currently over £16,500 per year.

gave a masterclass training to executives at a Chartered Institute of Housing conference on tackling the economic inequalities of Britain today, based on the research in the book *The spirit level - Why greater equality makes societies stronger.* [30]

But it was only on being elected as a City Councillor, and then becoming Mayor of Cambridge, that Terry saw a side of the city that tourists never see. It has never been an industrial city and there are pockets of real deprivation. The main employer has always been the University, which doesn't pay very high wages to its cooks, clerks, gardeners, porters, bedmakers, cleaners and other non-academic staff. Low wages and large numbers of students mean Cambridge has always had a shortage of decent accommodation at affordable rent.

In our years at the City Council, we have come across countless cases of overcrowding and people paying high rents for poor accommodation that landlords are often loath to keep in good repair. In Terry's earlier years, three quarters of all complaints brought to him were about housing. The Council has done its best to provide secure council homes at reasonable rents, but has often been hamstrung by conditions imposed by central government. And the pressures are even greater now. Cambridge's outrageous property prices mean people who work here often have to live fifty miles away, where prices are lower.

Unlike Terry, Diana didn't grow up in Cambridge: she is an incomer, a comparatively late arrival. She grew up in outer London, the land of suburbia, and then lived in inner London, part of a diverse and dynamic community. As a community activist and London Borough Councillor, it was no shock to her, on moving to Cambridge, to find that this too is a city of contrasts and conundrums.

The town of Cambridge is squeezed between the University's colleges, so need and deprivation weave in and out through prosperity, and around its edges. This is an ever-growing, thriving, successful city but - like

---

[30] Cited in footnote 26 on page 231.

everywhere else in this country of inequalities and contrasts - it holds many who have been left behind, struggling to make ends meet with low-paid, insecure jobs or no jobs at all.

Whether native English or incomers, they are now suffering from the cumulative cutbacks in services and support imposed by a central government that takes no thought or blame for the consequences of 'austerity'. In Diana's work at Cambridge Women's Resources Centre and in her volunteer roles, she sees daily the concrete consequences of this divide. She encounters the reality of those who are 'on the edge' outside prosperity and security, striving to survive against the backdrop of a housing crisis, welfare cuts, domestic abuse...

This book's speakers have gone through all of that and more, having escaped the nightmare of life-changing moments in their home country and reaching asylum here not to make a fortune or improve their status, but just to survive. Many of them who have been here for some time were able back then to avail of services and support that have now disappeared through lack of government funding (not through lack of need or demand!). For instance, the English language classes that Cambridge Women's Resources Centre were able to provide for Ruth in chapter one no longer exist.

Marella Hoffman has delicately opened the doors that give us insights into these eleven lives, as well as into her own journey. And now we are left wondering: what happened next? Because the stories told here are our stories too: everyone's survival is a cause for celebration, and an ongoing work in progress.

The final story - Kanwar's - a later addition, left us particularly moved and admiring and hopeful for his future. Here, in the mud of a vast tented camp, Kanwar reminds us of the depth of humanity that we are all capable of. Here we meet the contrast between two worlds again: between all of us here in Cambridge, whoever we are - and his little family, just about surviving in the mud of the camp, with no real guarantee of getting to anywhere safe. But amidst odds that would defeat most of us, Kanwar is able to forge friendship and collaboration with us through the written word, sending us this message: *You know, to live just for oneself must be a terrible existence. I always think: 'Give your life for something much larger than yourself. Live for a greater reality. Leave a legacy...'*

This book and its stories inspire us all to to do just that, working together to rebuild our civil solidarities in the uncertain times ahead.

Cambridge, January 2017

Appendix

A programme of policy actions to empower communities

Below is the programme of policy actions that were implemented based on insights gathered from the refugees and other migrants consulted during the outreach for this book. I, Marella Hoffman, delivered this work alongside a team of local authority professionals and community volunteers. These strategies and resources can be used by anyone interested in doing oral history with refugees or migrants to improve public policy and service provision, or using qualitative research to design a practical programme of policy actions for any other community. The programme of policy actions that we implemented had five levels, explained in detail below:

- community training workshops for the host community

- cultural education with the host community

- municipal publications

- political representation for ethnic communities

- preventive support for individuals

Community training workshops for the host community

- A specialist theatre company provided diversity training through humorous role-play, using audience interactions to break down prejudice. They used insights we had gleaned from the refugees' interviews to give an anti-racist and diversity training to an audience of 80 predominantly White English social housing tenants.

- An interactive workshop for the same demographic used role-reversal games around migration and ethnicity, with local authority staff and managers participating as well.

- A challenging training on racism, diversity and equality was given to a conference of social housing tenants from all over the East of England, organised by the UK's Chartered Institute of Housing. One of this book's refugee interviewees co-delivered the workshop with me, to an audience of primarily White English residents

- A master-class training was given to social housing managers at a conference of the Chartered Institute of Housing, as explained on page 235.

Cultural education with the host community

- Settled migrants contacted through our outreach project were supported to create an ethnic exhibition for the social housing community around them, with stalls sharing artefacts, traditions and gifts of cuisine from their cultures.

- A 'treasure trail' motivated the audience to visit and interact with every stall-holder at this exhibition, in order to qualify for a prize draw afterwards.

- Ethnic residents gave a traditional, costumed performance of the Chinese Dragon Dance to this audience, and one of the refugee interviewees from this book gave a talk.

Municipal publications

- A myth-busting series was published in the municipal magazine, debunking popular misconceptions about the numbers of migrants in the city, in social housing and on benefits.

- Articles factually corrected the myth that migrants get preferential treatment over native English, and raised awareness of the civic contributions they make.

- The magazine carried features about ethnic residents who were making a civic contribution and leading inspiring lives.

Political representation for ethnic communities:

I was employed by the local authority at that time to train and capacity-build poorer communities to participate in the democratic process. My task was to train them up through first forming residents' associations and receiving small community grants, then being consulted on the design of public services and finally, running for election to public office where they would help oversee public budgets of more than £30 million a year. We set ourselves targets for having people from poorer ethnic communities represented at each of the levels above. Through active outreach and making the roles more culturally welcoming, we achieved those targets.

Three Black women contacted through our ethnic outreach project worked their way up to being elected onto City Council decision-making boards, with equal voting rights alongside the politicians. In the course of their work, they pointed out that the city should have a specific Ethnic Minority Housing Strategy. But who knew the needs of these communities well enough to draw one up? The ethnic representatives were enlisted to help create the strategy, and to officially monitor that it got properly implemented. These are examples of oral history for public policy functioning as a 'ladder of participation', enabling excluded communities to eventually gain equal status alongside decision-makers. [31]

Preventive support for individuals

Seven of this book's interviewees had raised to me a specific problem they needed help with. For all these, we arranged personal follow-up with appropriate support services. Examples included needing:

- housing better adapted to their health needs
- a volunteering opportunity that would yield a good employment reference
- support in applying for jobs that reflected their advanced qualifications
- treatment for depression
- an intervention to restrain bullying neighbours

---

[31] A simpler version of this concept was first launched by Sherry Arnstein's 1969 article in the US entitled 'A ladder of citizen participation'.

- coaching on budgeting and managing their personal finances

All seven resolved those problems successfully with modest assistance, living more integrated lives as a result. For instance Ruth, from the opening chapter, was completely illiterate and could only sign her name as 'X'. She asked for help in learning some basic reading and writing, and the Cambridge Women's Resources Centre was able to provide a free literacy class where she quickly mastered reading and writing, enabling her to advance her roles in the several cleaning-companies she worked for.

Support services like these were at that time available to any resident of the city who needed them, as part of a well-planned strategy by local government and non-governmental support services to invest in early prevention. Small interventions like these help keep vulnerable residents housed, independent, employed, solvent and law-abiding - avoiding the much bigger public-finance costs of picking up the pieces around residents who become homeless, unemployed, destitute or involved in anti-social behaviour.

Climbing the ladder of civic participation

As seen above, the kind of empowerment work we did in Cambridge follows a known progression that is mapped out in academic theory as the 'ladder of civic participation'. It builds progressive up-skilling and autonomy, nurturing generative learning as individuals gather new abilities, and then spread them back into their communities. Versions of this 'road-map' can lift a group or community up through organised structures of influence in three broad stages:

- *first, the most grassroots organising:* e.g. from coffee-mornings in a block of flats to forming a residents' association in a housing estate or suburb

- *then, consultative levels:* where volunteers get experience representing their communities' interests on consultation boards that influence public services, from policing to street-cleaning, medical services to schools

- *finally, entering the democratic process*: experienced resident volunteers stand for election to public office and roles, taking on shared, official responsibility for how public funding is spent and community issues are addressed

In Cambridge, we expanded Arnstein's 'ladder of participation' into a more ambitious, detailed model that particularly emphasised the proactive spread of exponential learning *across* communities as they organised. Our local government had the commitment, values and funding to let us support communities and individuals over a number of years as they steadily worked their way up this Cambridge version of the civic ladder.

We used this ladder's steps not as some idealistic academic theory but as a pragmatic framework that residents from poorer and ethnic communities could and did actually move up through, mastering each level before they moved on to the next. These are the nine levels of opportunity and involvement that we facilitated for them, which can be - and have been - imported and adapted for use with other communities.[32]

1. *Public image*: First, ethnic and excluded communities need to see themselves reflected positively in the public discourse of an institution before they will ever approach that institution. This means positive, receptive images of that community in the institution's publications, brochures and outreach.

2. *Atmosphere*: Staff must make encounters culturally sensitive, warm and welcoming so that staff's personal manner, body language, dress code and way of speaking put the person at ease rather than being an obstacle.

3. *Empowerment*: After building more trusting relationships comes empowerment, where you start to give the community tools and resources they can make use of, such as trainings, work experience,

---

[32] This work in Cambridge has been published as a positive practice case study by the British government, and taught as a positive practice model to fifteen other local authorities around the country.

grants, equipment, projects to work on, supported experience at public speaking, etc.

4. *Consultation:* Next you give them official consultative roles, training and supporting them to sit confidently at decision-making tables where they are consulted, make a contribution and have a visible influence.

5. *Becoming trainers:* Now you can support them to give training sessions to their local peers in turn, passing on their own learnings in a cycle of generative learning.

6. *Wider self-training networks:* Then support them to join regional and national peer-networks, so they can eventually give trainings to their peers in other places, exchanging insights and empowerments with them.

7. *Devolving budgets:* Now you can devolve appropriate budgets for them to co-manage transparently as a responsible peer-group.

8. *Elected office:* Finally, you can train and empower them to stand for more formal elected roles as community representatives, and eventually for public office in the city, county or region alongside elected politicians.

9. *Paid employment:* Some residents may also graduate into paid professional employment as community organisers or leaders, as did one Black woman who engaged with our outreach project. After climbing the ladder above and being elected to public office alongside city councillors, she went on to take up a paid job in community development.

Some resources

The *Community Oral History Toolkit,* edited by Nancy Mackay and published by Routledge, is the most comprehensive collection of *How To* manuals on doing oral history with demographics like ethnic minorities, youth and elders, and planning and curating such projects.

Doing oral history - A practical guide, Donald Ritchie, Oxford Oral History Series, 2014 is a more general guide for doing oral history projects.

Making Voices Count - Reviewing practice in tenant involvement and empowerment, 2011, is the government publication that showcased our Cambridge community engagement work alongside other positive practice projects from around England.

Using oral history to improve public policies and programmes, my book published by Routledge in 2017, gives very detailed, hands-on instruction and case studies for doing this sort of work. It also sits in the University of East London's Living Refugee Archive as a companion volume to this present book.

For support, feedback or questions, you can email me any time at contact@marellahoffman.com or visit www.marellahoffman.com

The Living Refugee Archive at the University of East London can be contacted at library-archives@uel.ac.uk or by visiting www.livingrefugeearchive.org

About the author

Marella Hoffman has lectured or held research awards at universities in France, Switzerland, Ireland, the US and at Cambridge University. A Fellow of the Royal Anthropological Institute, she has worked extensively with aspects of government, using applied ethnography and contemporary oral history to circumvent conflict and generate policy solutions. As
well as writing for academic publishers, she was for a decade chief editor of a public policy magazine in Cambridge, communicating policy to the poorer communities affected by it, with a circulation of 40,000 copies per year.

Inspired by a psychoanalysis completed with a Fellow of Cambridge University, her work draws on the power of oral culture and dialogue. Her research has been published in collaborative international books such as *Location and Dislocation - Emigration and Irish Identities; Human Rights and Good Governance - Building Bridges;* and *Cross-Currents in European Literature.* Her solo books include the ethnography *Savoir-faire of the Elders - Green knowledge in the French Mediterranean hills* (Cahiers de la Salce and La Sorbonne University with Onslaught Books, written and published in French only). Her book *Using oral history to improve public policies and programmes* is published by Routledge across the English-speaking world in 2017.

For publications or to contact her, visit www.marellahoffman.com

Printed in Great Britain
by Amazon